LEADERS
FOR TOMORROW
EDITED BY ERIC VOGT AND ROBIN GRUMMAN-VOGT

inter(lass

Beaver's Pond Press, Inc.

ISBN 10: 1-59298-254-9
ISBN 13: 978-1-59298-254-7

Library of Congress Catalog Number: 2008938176

Printed in the United States of America

First Printing: 2009

12 11 10 09 08   5 4 3 2 1

Beaver's Pond Press, Inc.

Beaver's Pond Press, Inc.
7104 Ohms Lane, Suite 101
Edina, MN 55439–2129
(952) 829-8818
www.BeaversPondPress.com

to order, visit www.BookHouseFulfillment.com
or call 1-800-901-3480. Reseller discounts available.

This book is dedicated to all the members of the InterClass network for the past 17 years who contributed their energy and ideas to our collective understanding of leadership in this century! It is also dedicated with gratitude to the people who helped write this book including the many chapter authors. In particular, we are grateful to InterClass staff and friends, most notably Susan Saltrick, Louise Domenitz, Philip Kadish, and Kate O'Keefe, who made significant suggestions for format, ideas, and organization that enabled this book to be completed.

InterClass wishes to thank the organizations that have been members of the InterClass Network during its 17 year history. Included among these are:

American Express	Lancaster University
AT&T	Los Alamos National Labs
Bell Labs	Microsoft
BT	Pfizer Pharmaceuticals
BP	Prudential Financial
CIBC	Prudential UK
Chevrolet	Saturn Corporation
Chevron	Shell Oil
CSC	Skandia
Deloitte	Swedish Post
Dupont	Unilever
Granite Construction	UTC/Otis Elevator
Honeywell	Department of Veterans Affairs
Institute for Research on Learning	Volvo
KPMG	Xerox

CONTENTS

Part I Views on Leadership from the InterClass Network

ABOUT INTERCLASS

InterClass is a consulting firm focusing on innovations at the intersection of business strategy and human performance. Founded in 1990, our work enables the emergence of leaders and business models, which support high performing, sustainable organizations. This book developed as a result of our years of individual company consulting, and particularly is the fruit of nearly two decades of intensive multi-company conferences on topics impacting leadership.

InterClass conducts leadership sessions with individual consulting clients around the world, and hosts an annual conference of business leaders from top companies in many industries.

For many years, InterClass conducted in-depth conferences throughout the year with participants attending a number of conferences and joining an on-going network of business leaders addressing group concerns on leadership as well as other critical business issues. We now hold a single annual conference, which allows business leaders to continue the highly-valued work they do together while acknowledging the acceleration of virtual networking in today's business world.

The InterClass purpose and processes are the same, whether focused on a single consulting client or applied to a conference of leaders from a number of companies. The InterClass processes are interactive and transformative. These processes are described in detail in the second section of this text entitled: The InterClass Process.

InterClass welcomes your responses to this book. To speak with InterClass regarding this book, to discuss possible consulting relationship with InterClass, or to inquire regarding conference attendance, please contact us:

(617) 864-5300

www.**interclass**.com

ABOUT THE EDITORS

Eric E. Vogt

Co-Founder and President, InterClass

Eric E. Vogt is a business catalyst, educator, and entrepreneur, whose passion is igniting new possibilities for others. By leading individuals and organizations on journeys that begin with visioning and result in accelerated growth, he has created positive transformational experiences for large organizations, educational institutions, entrepreneurial ventures, and non-profits alike. Vogt is uniquely able to identify and harness today's potential to fuel tomorrow's growth.

Vogt's work focuses primarily on generating fresh insights, facilitating innovation, and then developing the business strategies as well as developing the capacity of the leadership teams to achieve that future. He began his business career with The Boston Consulting Group, where over a period of seven years he developed strategies for clients ranging from major manufacturing firms to Sweden's Ministry of Industry. Subsequently, he joined the faculty of the Harvard Business School where he taught international economics in the MBA program. In 1983, Vogt founded MicroMentor, Inc., an award-winning firm in the design and development of interactive multimedia learning. When MicroMentor merged with Omega Performance in 1997, Vogt became Omega's chief learning officer. Vogt left Omega in 1999 to found Communispace Corporation. Communispace creates and facilitates private, online communities that engage influential customers, generate fresh insights, and dramatically increase marketing effectiveness.

In 1990, Vogt co-founded InterClass, a research consortium and applied consulting practice focused upon innovations at the intersection of business strategy and human performance. Currently, Vogt's primary activities are devoted to the InterClass agenda, exploring and applying new perspectives and novel processes to enhance corporate performance. Over the past five years, he has devoted his energy to leadership team development and accelerated cultural change in global organizations across various industries including consumer products, pharmaceuticals, consulting, education, and financial services.

Along with his entrepreneurial and business ventures, Vogt has been at the helm of several organizations where he has been instrumental in establishing innovative new directions. Vogt served as founder and two-term president of the Massachusetts Computer Software Council, vice chair of the Board of Bay State Skills Corporation, founder of the Belmont Second Soccer League, and overseer of the Boston Museum of Science. He is a member of the Common Angels, a high-tech seed capital group developing young entrepreneurs. Earlier in his career, Lt. Vogt served as the CIC officer aboard the USS Dewey (DLG-14), seeing combat action in Da Nang and in the Gulf of Tonkin during the Vietnam War.

Vogt earned an MBA with distinction from Harvard Business School and graduated cum laude from Harvard College with a BA in linguistics and applied mathematics. He is fluent in English, Spanish, and French.

Robin Grumman-Vogt

Senior Director, InterClass

Robin Grumman-Vogt is an accomplished consultant, facilitator and designer of innovative learning experiences for corporations and educational businesses. She facilitates the generation of new insights and actions out of the hopes and fears that stem from change. Her recent work includes the design and rollout of a stakeholder analysis process for the European division of a Pharmaceutical client grappling with the loss of "the doctor" focus for their sales and marketing efforts. The process Robin designed empowered the organization to identify and build relationships with a broad array of new and influential stakeholders.

Earlier in her career, Robin spent a decade working in financial services, first as the vice-president of advisory services at Chase Manhattan Bank, and then as director of organization development at the Bank of Boston. During this period of change in the Banking industry, Robin worked to introduce technology as a core strategic lever and as a pivotal component of financial product design. At Chase Manhattan, Robin's early responsibilities included marketing and training strategies for new technology-delivered finance products, such as the first automated Letter of Credit System. At the end of her seven-year tenure at Chase, Robin was managing a multi-million dollar department responsible for a broad array of internally-offered consulting services including change management consulting, personal computing strategy and systems training. Robin was responsible for a multi-year initiative called "Technology and Bank," designed to enable Chase executives around the globe to understand and engage technology as a part of all business and product strategies. At the Bank of Boston, Robin continued to focus on changes in the financial services industry. With the growth of American banks across state boundaries, Robin lead the effort to use new learning technologies to train large geographically dispersed populations of employees. During her tenure at Bank of Boston, Robin was also responsible for Human Resource Planning and Employee Surveys focusing on the emerging understanding of the importance of Talent in our organizations.

Robin then spent several years as a sales executive and consultant for three firms in the arena of educational software: MicroMentor, Omega Performance and Avaltus. During this time she focused on empowering multiple organizations to use new learning technologies. Robin holds a BA degree in Political Science from Hunter College, and an MBA from New York University.

FOREWORD

"No problem can be solved from the same consciousness that created it. We must learn to see the world anew."
—**Albert Einstein**

In the century past, the health, wealth, and general happiness of the citizens of all nations were based upon purely extractive industries and occasional industrial brilliance. If you were a country with oil, iron ore, copper ore, gold, bauxite, waterpower, or vast productive farmlands, you fared well in the scheme of the world economy. Alternatively, if you made the right investments over a long period of time, like Japan or Korea, you could bootstrap your way towards the top of the economic heap.

For the future, however, these simple economic strategies are not sufficient.

Can we really expect the kind of leadership that brought us here to have a prayer of leading us out? Probably not. Given the nature of the challenges we are facing, *creative leadership* will be required both at the country and organizational level. Like the quote from Einstein suggests, we need leaders who will see the world anew, and think and act at higher levels of consciousness. It follows that now, more than ever, we need a fresh perspective on how to identify and develop our leaders.

A few examples of creative leadership, at the country and business level, are worth considering.

In 1950, Singapore was so poor that its leaders went to Malaysia to ask them to acquire the country and provide for the people. Malaysia's leaders declined, saying that it would be too much of a burden. Lee Kwan Yu, formerly a communist labor union leader, had the vision to reform the institutions, adopt democracy and capitalism, and, most importantly, to invest in the education of the people. Today Singapore is a vibrant agricultural and knowledge economy, which ranks in the world's top ten in terms of GNP per capita.

In 1947 an oppressive military dictator was running Costa Rica. José Figueres, better known as "Don Pepe," an agricultural entrepreneur, economist, and philosopher, led a popular armed revolt, ousting the military government. Once legitimately elected, Figueres proceeded to abolish the military and declare that Costa Rica would invest those resources in education instead. Intel recently located a major semiconductor plant in Costa Rica, based upon access to skilled labor. Costa Rica now boasts a standard of living that is four times greater than the average for all of Latin America.

In terms of business leaders, John McFarlane, retiring CEO of ANZ Bank in Australasia is an example of the kind of high integrity, creative leader the business world is requiring. John McFarlane was brought into ANZ from the outside in 1997 after the bank experienced several years of poor performance. However, issues of financial performance were but the tip of the iceberg. In Australia in the 90s, banks were regarded with widespread mistrust due to years of branch closings and fee increases. McFarlane faced ill will from ANZ customers, employees, and the communities in which the bank operated. In his ten years at ANZ he undertook a three-part plan that equally addressed the concerns of all three of the above stakeholder groups. A significant part of his mission was to turn ANZ into "the bank with a human face." This cultural transformation moved ANZ

- From bureaucracy and hierarchy to meritocracy
- From controlling information to openness and trust
- From a silo mentality to collaboration
- From cost reduction to a focus on customers and values
- From cost-cutting to growth through innovation (including cost management)

McFarlane is known for saying "Breakout, be bold and have the courage to be different. We try new things, rethink our old ways, set stretching goals and achieve them, and we constantly challenge ourselves to create and deliver sustainable value over the long-term." And the results at ANZ support his actions.

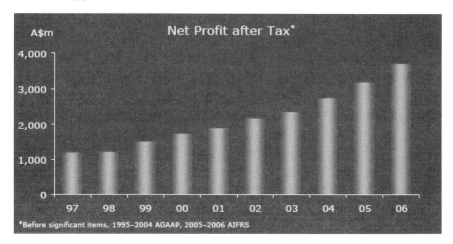

2006 Annual report—taken from ANZ website

Irreverent may not be a descriptor you would expect of a business leader never mind the CEO of Pepsi! But that is exactly how Indra Nooyi, CEO of PepsiCo since 2006, is described in a recent *Business Week* article.[1] Former Pepsi CEO Roger Enrico says of Nooyi, "Indra can drive as deep and hard as anyone I've ever met, but she can do it with a sense of heart and fun." She advocated for some business choices that were not obvious winners—including spinning off Taco Bell, KFC, and Pizza Hut, arguing PepsiCo couldn't bring enough value to the fast food industry. She is also noted for promoting the concept of "performance with purpose," aiming to make PepsiCo a leader in offering healthy foods and hiring a diverse workforce. Business week describes her as "comfortable enough with her leadership presence to patrol the office barefoot at times and even sing in the halls, perhaps a holdover from her teen days in an all-girl rock band in her hometown of Chennai, India." Nooyi demonstrates enormous authenticity and social responsibility while exercising proficient business savvy.

---

1.   June 11, 2007, *Business Week*, "Indra Nooyi: Keeping Cool in Hot Water"

Nooyi joined PepsiCo in 1994 and became CFO in 2001. Since she became CFO, the company's annual revenues have risen 72%, while net profit more than doubled, to $5.6 billion in 2006. Admirable performance with purpose.

These are examples of creative, visionary leaders who have made a lasting difference for their countries and businesses. The country leaders took on a complex system, held a strong vision, made significant investments in education, and looked at the long term. The business leaders have demonstrated the capacity to innovate and inspire with integrity on a global basis. They have also continued to demonstrate historically valued leadership attributes such as promoting trust and avoiding the repetition of past mistakes.

The thesis of this book is that we need more leaders with bold and creative capability AND these leaders need to continue to demonstrate leadership behaviors that have always been needed and valued. The new generation of leaders needed to carry the torch of tomorrow are being educated and groomed today—in your organizations. This book is a contribution to those leaders and to you who are mentoring, coaching, and developing them. It is different than the other books on leadership in several ways.

First, it does not look to the mythic male hero (the FDRs, the JFKs or the Jack Welchs) as the model. Rather than the traditional male hero, for the future we are likely looking at leaders who demonstrate more balance, flexibility (dare we say more "feminine"), and comfortable with a broader range of behaviors —leaders who are emotionally intelligent, inclusive, group-oriented, reflective; leaders who have peripheral vision, storytelling skills, advanced network competence, and the ability to ignite productive and transformative conversations. We believe in leaders who listen as well as and possibly more than they speak. These leaders are the torch carriers for the future.

Second, this book looks at leadership as more of a verb than a noun. What are the actions of the leaders we need for tomorrow, not simply who are the leaders we need for tomorrow? What are the stories that characterize these leaders? What are the business imperatives that suggest the nature of this emerging breed?

Third, this book describes "not throwing the baby out with the bath water." There are many leadership practices that have always been required, some on a daily basis. These practices must continue in the new creative leaders if they are to succeed. Through descriptions of the Inter-Class process we use in our consortia and consulting meetings, many of these behaviors are surfaced and valued; important though they are, some, like the essential air we breathe, have become invisible to us.

Finally, and perhaps most important, this book is written by actual practitioners— line leaders and development professionals—external consultants and internal catalysts—who are committed to supporting leaders who can think and envision at a different level than those who have led our world to the threshold of this new century. In fact, this book is written by the consulting clients, consortium members, staff, and network of associates that are InterClass.

InterClass the consortium, which was co-founded in 1990 by Eric Vogt and Dr. Jim Botkin, has been a unique high-trust network of experienced professionals from large corporations; actively searching for insight and innovations at the intersection of business strategy and human performance. We aim our work to enable the emergence of leaders and business models, which support high performing, sustainable organizations. Our mission has remained the same but the organization has evolved into three parts—a consulting practice, catalytic conference offerings in consortia or for specific clients, and a synergistic network of practitioners. Those involved with InterClass are all explorers, innovators, and implementers, actively engaged in the development of large-scale organizational changes and capability development. We operate as a high-trust global network, linked by our passion for innovation and a pursuit of a radically better tomorrow.

This book and the way it is written is itself reflective of creative new-style leadership. This book is a collaborative effort; it respects the wisdom of multiple perspectives, and it models an ongoing conversation. In some places it may raise more questions than provide answers, because we know that seeking the right question is usually the most important work of a leader.

INTRODUCTION

Our world today is very different from the one into which we were born, offering a host of new challenges and opportunities. On the one hand, we see an emerging global knowledge economy fed by an unprecedented investment in network technologies and the unleashing of human creativity in all fields. The genomic revolution, in particular, promises very real breakthroughs in science, health, agriculture, and business. For those of us fortunate enough to participate in this emerging economy, the future is both bright and energizing.

At the same time, we also face significant challenges. Global Warming. AIDS. Economic Disparity—between the developed and the developing world and between the poor, the middle class, and the wealthy in the developing world. Global Terrorism. Health Care Crises. Education Inadequacies. Religious Intolerance. When we encounter and engage these problems the future feels insecure and downright frightening.

Today's leaders and those who are just emerging—in fact those who are being developed as you read this paragraph—will be the ones who must deal with both of these realities and set the course for the future. The leadership thinking of previous eras created the challenges today's leaders face, but that thinking won't solve them. An old adage holds that to the man with a hammer, every problem looks like a nail. Today's leaders need a new toolbox.

Are the leaders in your organization ready? Are you having the conversations you need to have in your organization to make them ready?

The InterClass Process is meant to foment and nurture those conversations. It aims to not only get your organization ready for the current challenges and opportunities, but to develop a dynamic process within your organization that will continue to evolve in response to the inevitable changes to come.

The Views presented in the first part of this compendium contain the results of interactions on leadership the InterClass Process has generated. We invite you to both delve into these historic results and engage in new conversations in your own organizations.

Part I

Views on Leadership from the InterClass Network

Part I Overview

Different Intellectual Fruit from the Same Seed

InterClass represents a marvelous web of people, in both its consulting form (practitioners and clients) and consortium form (staff and members). That web includes internal company executives and external consultants with backgrounds ranging from HR and IT to organization development and marketing to product innovation and learning. Many individuals within the broad InterClass network have held very diverse positions across time. Several internal corporate executives within the network have done a turn as consultants—sometimes switching back and forth multiple times. We have had members who held positions stressing varied domains of expertise: former OD consultants who held internal corporate positions focused primarily on product innovation, for example. The InterClass network includes individuals with equal capacity to hold positions in either marketing, IT, or strategy! This diversity of expertise *within* individuals matched by the diversity of thinking *between* individuals in the network enables our collective conversations to spawn diverse perspectives: different intellectual fruit from the same seed.

Hence, InterClass does not represent a single vision of leadership. (Though there are many concepts and beliefs that a consensus might well exist about across the network—for example, we suspect there is a consensus that the demands on leadership are changing and expanding.) Rather InterClass represents a series of conversational, interactive, and iterative processes that have generated interconnected and diverse thinking on the topic of leadership. The chapters in this section represent these thoughts. While Liedtka, Mota, Wenger, Swain, and Henschel, for example, talk about very different components of leadership, the connections between them are quite visible in shared vocabulary and metaphors. Using Mota's work as a jumping off place:

- he uses the communities of practice label coined by Henchel's organization, IRL

- talks about the "design" requirements of his metaphoric white water rafts mirroring the importance of the leader as designer stressed in Liedtka's work
- Wenger's comments about business, unlike chess, never coming to an end are mirrored by Mota's comments on transcendent leadership not having an end point
- Mota's points on the need for permeable open networks of relationships are mirrored in the network chapters by both EE Vogt and Swain.

This is who we are: a network of practitioners both inside and consulting to organizations, improving each of our unique practices through shared conversation. Our sincere hope is that you, the reader, will benefit from the content and model of this conversation, carry it into your own endeavors and conversations, and perhaps even join ours.

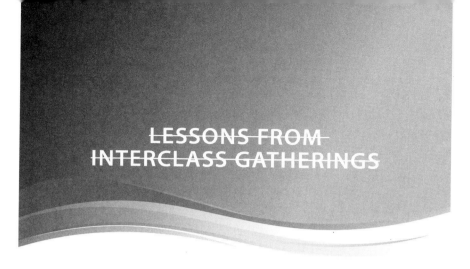

LESSONS FROM INTERCLASS GATHERINGS

By Robin Grumman-Vogt

Leadership has been the most frequented topic in the history (1990—2007) of InterClass. InterClass has witnessed the rise and fall of any number of ideas about leadership. Management books—and the theories that spawn them—seem to age as quickly as the fashion page. Yet, looking back over our own conference notes, we see some surprisingly enduring themes. We wonder if these themes endure because they represent issues that we have yet to resolve or if they represent a need to build consensus to a tipping point—to a point that enables action. Because of the enduring nature of some of these themes we have noted occasional skepticism among InterClass participants and clients around what it takes to achieve full implementation across our organizations and society of well documented leadership development capacities. For example, how many leadership developers need to hold the perspective that personal aspects of a leaders life need to be included in leadership programs before the personal becomes a component of leadership efforts in the majority of our organizations? As we will discuss further below, InterClass holds—from both its consulting practice and consortium meetings—that the effectiveness of leadership development is greatly heightened when the emotions and their roots in personal experience are included. This belief has remained controversial in the years of our practice, and yet the majority of practitioners in our contact and reading believe in its efficacy.

Even back in 1993, InterClass held a conference hosted by KPMG Peat Marwick and American Express that focused on new approaches to executive development. At that conference, people talked about:

- Changing the emphasis in our view of leadership—away from being mostly about business, a little on leadership, and not much at all on the personal, to a more equal distribution of energy among the three.
- Connecting learning and leadership—that a primary leadership responsibility was creating and stimulating a culture of learning
- Shifting responsibility for executive development—from being solely an HR function to a critical task of the CEO.

Not only is personal content still a point of contention in leadership development conversations today, but so are the topics of leadership owning the development of their people both at the top and throughout the organization by fostering a culture of learning.

The next year, in 1994, one of the InterClass conferences was hosted by the Center for Creative Leadership in North Carolina and the World Bank in Washington, D.C. There we were surrounded by world-renowned thinkers on leadership who explored with us the new work of leaders, including:

- Leading as influencers and meaning makers, rather than dominators
- Shifting from an industrial-age emphasis on the size and power of the organization to a human-centered organization focused on innovation and engagement
- Getting work done through informal networks
- Using intuitive thinking and metaphors to spur organizational learning
- Finding time for reflection in the midst of relentless change.

Again, all of these topics are still active in our leadership development design conversations today. The need for organizations to focus on innovation and employee engagement as sustainable advantages occupies a considerable portion of the InterClass consulting practice today. And that may be the notable difference. In 1994 we **talked** about the importance of the influencers of engagement and innovation. Today InterClass is helping organizations **implement** strategies around engagement and innovation that enable corporate leaders to create sustainable business models.

Those same ideas cropped up again in a 1997 meeting with the PIPSA Group in Cuernavaca, Mexico, plus other related topics such as:

- Rising globalization and open markets—and what this interdependence means
- Shifting from cheap to productive labor through the development of human capital
- Understanding the role of emotion in a knowledge-driven workplace
- Fostering social responsibility in emerging and developed economies
- Using powerful conversations as a means of effecting change.

Globalization issues have grown and labor shifts remain core to this topic. As demonstrated by the high interest in the work InterClass has done in its consulting practice on changes to the picture of globalization, hunger for greater understanding of global factors continues to increase. Similarly, corporate social responsibility has exploded since 1997 as a focal point for business leadership as demonstrated by the proliferation of business titles on this topic, from Grayson and Hodges' "Corporate Social Opportunity" to Laszlo's "The Sustainable Company" to Jackson and Nelson's "Profits with Principles" and many, many more.

In 2002, in the Basque country, hosted by the Mondragon Group, the largest cooperative in the world, InterClass explored the roles of leaders in new organizational structures. As technology extended reach, collapsed distance, and dissolved management layers, leadership no longer dwelt only at the top of the organization—instead, it was distributed across self-emergent, often ad hoc, networks. In a world where intellectual capital was becoming the primary measure of value, leaders resembled teachers and coaches. The metaphors in the air reflected a new era of turbulent change—leaders as designers, as dancers, as stewards, as servants—in which the leader sought to find the creative edge between order and chaos. All of this beautifully builds upon the need for leaders to nurture the learning of everyone in their organizations covered in the 1993 InterClass conference.

Maybe this is the important point—our ideas are not lying unresolved they are being understood more deeply and applied more broadly. The need for continued discussion is not driven by an absence of resolve but a need for motivation and fuel to deepen practice.

Thus, in April 2005, the Department of Veterans Affairs hosted our meeting on "Developing Tomorrow's Leaders." We explored how leadership development was changing—and needed to change still further—to address the realities of today's business environment and characteristics of the new generation of workers. Among our conclusions, were the following key insights:

- Leadership development needs to better reflect & support the actual work of the organization.
- We need to move from creating events to creating an ongoing sustained process for development.
- Facilitating self-awareness and emotional awareness in future leaders is key.

As we look at these lists of themes from past conferences, we may experience some déjà vu. Indeed are our leadership development efforts advancing sufficiently? When we narrow the scope of our measurements, I think these questions come into focus with an appreciative response. No, fostering organization-wide learning is not a competence universally expected of corporate leaders in 2007, but it is easy to find conversations on this question and cases of actual implementations of this competence in the present business literature. And isn't that what we need most— living questions and active conversations that are being applied? Yes, some topics from 1993 are still appearing in 2007 AND our increased learning on each topic is clearly demonstrated by the refinement of the conversations, the increase in the number of implementations, and the variety of participants engaging in conversations on these topics. For example, among the authors of the present Corporate Responsibility Literature are presidents of corporations, a former head of public relations for a financial services company, and professors from different disciplines ranging from science to business economics. This variety of sources and identification of successful implementations is enriching the inputs and outcomes of our leadership development efforts daily. We have learned a lot, and we want to continue to learn even more in order to successfully lead our way into a healthy future.

Effective leadership development has an impact on our individual organizations, but it also has an impact on society. At core, what we're trying to achieve is the transformation of our whole societal mindset about the leadership of business and societal enterprises such as corporations, government agencies, and NGOs. This isn't easy, and it won't happen overnight. Big recurring themes—the interconnection of our world, the acceleration of change, the complexity of modern life—all have a major impact on leaders and the organizations they lead. Indeed, the new work of leaders will never be done. As Malcolm Gladwell might say, the many successful efforts in leadership development keep building to new tipping points for change. Here at InterClass, we don't have all the answers, but we do ask some powerful questions in the presence of powerful minds. After all, the leader's role today is not one of answering, but one of asking.

As Rainer Maria Rilke said, "Live the questions now." That way, we live our way into the answers.

Lessons from the InterClass Process and Business History

The chapters about the InterClass process presented in this compendium profess that many actions that enable effective leadership are consistent throughout business history. For example, we believe that throughout time leaders have been well served by:

- promoting trust
- making norms of behavior explicit and attending to inconsistencies
- using surveys and other methods to understand the needs of all constituencies/stakeholders
- listening as well as speaking
- requesting and demonstrating preparation prior to meetings
- encouraging the documentation of decisions, events, and ideas (note taking)

- encouraging mentoring to create a legacy of knowledge
- matching environment to purpose
- using appreciation to develop and reinforce competence
- surfacing and challenging assumptions
- reviewing prior actions to avoid future pitfalls
- demonstrating respect for different perspectives
- preventing mental models from distorting information and decisions
- creating safe spaces to learn and innovate
- being thoughtful and non-reactive when moving to action.

However, most of these attributes can be demonstrated under very different styles of and missions for leadership, even ones that we would not condone today. Ways of leadership now abhorrent to us were often suited to their times and though the means are no longer acceptable to us the outcomes might well be admired today. Let's briefly look at business history at the time of the Gilded Age (1865–1914)—when the term "Robber Baron" was coined. A positive standout in this period was Charles Francis Adams Jr., the great-grandson of President John Adams and grandson of President John Q. Adams. After his time as a general in the Civil War, Charles Francis Adams was appointed to the Massachusetts Railroad Commission. His methods could be said to include:

- promoting trust
- making norms of behavior explicit and attending to inconsistencies
- using surveys and other methods to understand the needs of all constituencies/stakeholders
- listening as well as speaking
- encouraging the documentation of decisions, events, and ideas
- surfacing and challenging assumptions
- reviewing prior actions to avoid future pitfalls.

Adams' Railroad Commission was called the "Sunshine Commission" as it tried to bring corrupt business practices into the light of day in the belief that this would shame the Robber Barons into compliance with accepted business norms. He was also viewed as an excellent leader in his management of the Union Pacific Railroad from 1884 to 1890. And yet, Charles Francis Adams was, like the Robber Barons he tried to shame, a promoter of protecting business over consumers. His leadership in the field of regulation was focused on protecting "businessmen" from the public whose needs were viewed as both unrelenting and as changeable as the wind. In the light of today's views it is hard for us to see Charles Francis Adams, Jr. as a great leader of major reform, and yet he exhibited so many of the actions we would still view as indicators of effective leadership. And in his time he did indeed successfully lead an effort that achieved significant reform and resultant improvement in business governance.

What does the story of Charles Francis Adams teach us? Partly that being a "man of his time" enabled him to be successful in his time. It is likely that his views on "the public" would not enable Charles Adams to be successful today. Hence, the leaders of each day must artfully blend a mixture of changes to enable the future (regulatory reform in Adam's case) with past views (mistrust of the consumer in Adam's case) in order to arrive at the tipping point that moves us to the future. The story of Charles Francis Adams is also a reminder that every leader can only effectively be understood in the context of the history in which he lived.

So, What IS the context of leadership today? For the InterClass perspective on that question, see our next article, "Whole Leaders: A New Consciousness for Leadership in the 'Fourth Wave' Economy."

WHOLE LEADERS:

A New Consciousness for Leadership in the "Fourth Wave" Economy

By Eric E. Vogt and Robin Grumman-Vogt

Part One

Leadership in the Multi-Generational Workplace

"At present another composition is commencing, each generation has its composition, people do not change from one generation to another generation but the composition that surrounds them changes." [2]

~ Gertrude Stein ~

The wonderful quote from Gertrude Stein that opens this chapter suggests that the composition—or the context—that surrounds each generation is unique. Today's leaders are primarily a mix of the Baby Boomer and Gen X generations. They make for a powerful leadership combination. The Baby Boomers are a product of the history of their parents' generation—what Tom Brokaw has labeled as the Greatest Generation—those who grew up in the Great Depression and fought in World War II. The many trials they experienced led them to fully appreciate the extreme prosperity of the 1950s and beyond. With this perspective, the greatest generation infused their children with a sense of security that enabled Baby Boomers to rebel—in part because they believed that prosperity would always be there.

---

2. Stein, Gertrude. (1984). *Picasso*. New York: Courier Dover Publications.

Hence, as Richard Croker writes, Baby Boomers are "applauded for their idealism and attacked for their materialism, praised for their innovation and condemned for their rebelliousness."[3] There is no incongruence in this description as it depicts what Baby Boomers had to become given the surrounding composition provided by their parents. Erica Jong, the epoch defining novelist, believes the Baby Boomer generation also is particularly self-confident. As the offspring of parents who truly adored their children and were so thrilled to be through the war, they emerged into a prosperous world and replaced the many lives lost. Their bountiful self-confidence continues to enable a particular brand of dedication to purpose and resulting leadership success.[4]

Rosabeth Moss Kanter, in an interview about her 2005 book *Confidence: How Winning Streaks and Losing Streaks Begin and End*, talks about the importance of confidence to business success:

> Confidence is certainly mental, but it's not a mindset in the sense that it's always present. Confidence is a situational expectation—an expectation of a positive outcome. And that expectation leads to all kinds of investments in making that outcome come true. Because of confidence people put in the effort, they invest financial and other resources. Instead of giving up, they stay in the game longer and, therefore, have more chances to succeed. But it's not necessarily rooted in people's character. Some people may be more likely to develop confidence than others, but it's definitely a response to specific situations."[5]

The initial "specific situations" encountered by the Baby Boomers, adoring parents in a prosperous world, enabled a strong dedication to purpose, which continues to support Baby Boomers in their confidence especially when their efforts have been met with success. However, the

---

3. Croker, Richard. (2007). *The Boomer Century, 1946–2046*. New York: Springboard Press, p. XI.

4. Croker, Richard. (2007). *The Boomer Century, 1946–2046*. New York: Springboard Press, p. 9.

5. "Meet the Masterminds: Rosabeth Moss Kanter on Confidence, Management Consulting News," January (2005)

Baby Boomers initial grounding makes it more likely that even without consistent experience of success this generation has a higher propensity to keep "going for it."

The Gen Xers parented by Baby Boomers are, according to *Barron's Marketing Dictionary*, "characterized as having a high affinity for technology and as being computer and Internet proficient, skeptical about advertising claims, fast spending, and more impressed by personal style than designer price tags." Entrepreneurship is high among Generation Xers, and they tend to move easily from one employer to another. There is disagreement about the level of civic engagement of Gen Xers—we believe however that this disagreement is inflamed by the metrics used. In short, Baby Boomers have given more money to causes than any other generation. The Gen Xers, on the other hand, are not giving away as much money, but they may well be *doing* more for causes than any other generation. The Gen Xers seem willing to have their work pay less if it serves causes they believe in.

Again the commonly shared characteristics of Gen Xers make sense given the composition that they were surrounded by; most notably their Baby Boomer parents. As Howe and Strauss wrote in their recent HBR article,[6] "Gen Xers grew up in an era of failing schools and marriages, when the collective welfare of children sank to the bottom of the nation's priorities…so Xers learned early on to distrust institutions." Again a key demonstration of this is the high levels of entrepreneurship among the Gen Xers. Howe and Straus report that 3 out of 5 Gen Xers want to "be their own boss."[7]

So what does the present composition mean for the leadership mix of Baby Boomers and Generation Xers? The present context is evaporating the boundaries between business life and charitable endeavors. Doing good is no longer seen as a separate agenda from our work. In larger business environments this has spawned the rise of corporate social responsibility. The needs and operation of the corporation must be aligned with the social requirements of supporting broad purchasing and use of the products created and sold by corporations. So we are seeing corporations like Whirlpool

---

6. Howe, Neil, and Strauss, William. "The Next 20 Years: How Customer and Workforce Attitudes Will Evolve", *Harvard Business Review,* July–August 2005, p. 3

7. Howe, Neil, and Strauss, William. "The Next 20 Years: How Customer and Workforce Attitudes Will Evolve", *Harvard Business Review,* July–August 2005, p. 3

create strong partnerships with social support institutions that enable more people to inhabit homes that are optimized by their products. Since 1999, Whirlpool Corporation has contributed more than $34 million in donations and cash to support Habitat for Humanity's mission to eliminate poverty housing. Currently, Whirlpool donates a refrigerator and range to every new Habitat home built in North America. In addition, thousands of its employees volunteer to build Habitat homes every year.

The importance of the connection between our businesses and the charities they support is essential to the composition surrounding leadership today. As Michael Porter and Mark Kramer state in their December 2006 *Harvard Business Review* article, "An affirmative corporate social agenda moves from mitigating harm to reinforcing corporate strategy through social process."

The ease of connection enabled by the internet and supported by the technology capabilities of the Gen Xers, their ease of movement across employers and other environments, and the confidence and communicative skills of Baby Boomers all support the advent of social networks as a tool for creating constituencies that go beyond traditional boundaries. Who these leaders are leading is no longer restricted by conventional definitions of business manager, influential friend, or not-for-profit leader.

The bounds seem limitless in the potential for this mixed generation of leaders, but that does not guarantee that their leadership will result in good outcomes. After all, the Enron and Arthur Anderson scenarios and other recent ethical improprieties have come out of their leadership and the present context. Just as on the organizational level, the boundary between work and social action is blurring, so, too, on the individual level, the line between personal and corporate values is eroding. Ensuring that the beneficial attributes of this generational mix do the most good for the individual, society, and its institutions requires that our leaders are more conscious and in touch with their emotions, beliefs, and mental models and how they impact their organizations' decisions and actions. This has been the focus of much of the work of InterClass in its' consulting practice. InterClass refers to the present context as the "Fourth Wave" and the leadership development required for this wave as the "Whole Leader School."

Part Two

The Whole Leader School & the Fourth Wave

What are the qualities we need to nurture in our leaders and in ourselves *as leaders*? InterClass has developed a framework called, "The Fourth Wave" to describe the context in which leadership must effectively navigate today.

Post-World War II leadership has gone through four distinct periods. In the '50s and especially the '60s, the heyday of general management, companies were stable and hierarchical leadership forms prevailed. In business at this time the command and control structures and processes that "won the war," were very effective under a stable economy. In the '70s and '80s, economic pressures drove leaders to focus on their role as communicators of vision and strategy. The instability of the economy during this period, such as the stagflation and labor relation issues of the '70s, called for leaders who could use tools and resources for market analysis, strategy design, and corporate communication to empower and steer the enterprise through changing times. In the '90s, as global competition intensified, leaders sought competitive advantage by bridging boundaries of country and culture. Leaders needed the ability to design strategies that enabled members of the enterprise to operate together while in different places and different time zones. Now, in the first decade of a new millennium, we've arrived at the Fourth Wave—one of continuous change and creative foment in a flat world of interconnection and interdependence.

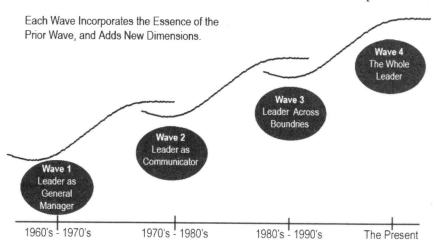

Each Wave Incorporates the Essence of the Prior Wave, and Adds New Dimensions.

Wave 1 — Leader as General Manager — 1960's - 1970's
Wave 2 — Leader as Communicator — 1970's - 1980's
Wave 3 — Leader Across Boundries — 1980's - 1990's
Wave 4 — The Whole Leader — The Present

Today's leaders must inspire, engage, and connect to maintain an innovative edge and engage the creativity of the entire workforce. Leadership is no longer a function of one person at the top, instead leadership is often distributed and fluid, shifting among places, people, and processes. The goals of leadership are different, too, from the command and control ethos of earlier periods. Today, leaders seek to inspire the workforce and the society around them, promote a culture of creativity, accelerate innovation, and ensure impeccable execution.

Now in the first decade of a new millennium, we've arrived at the Fourth Wave—one of continuous change and creative foment in a flat world of interconnection and interdependence.

How does a leader do this? The question might better be asked: How does a leader become this? The Whole Leader School of Development asserts that the effective leaders of tomorrow must integrate four dimensions of development: Intellectual, Emotional, Physical, and Meaningful.

Four Dimensions of Leadership

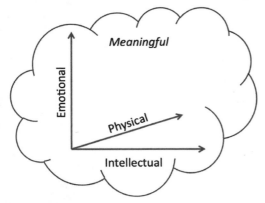

The application of each dimension requires both specific capabilities and willingness. These energies do not stand alone. They are often coupled or blended in order to effectively achieve a specific leadership action. But specific requirements of the leaders' role put demands on specific forms of energy.

PHYSICAL ENERGY

Physical energy is used by leaders when they actively demonstrate commitment. Today for leaders to be successful they must actively live the mission, vision, and values of their organizations. Their actions must be demonstrably coherent with the company's purpose, the future it desires, and the culture and ethics by which it wishes to get there. Examples of such actions include simple things like visibly celebrating significant contracts and alliances that move the mission forward. It also includes the making of complex decisions such as choosing to fire a senior executive who has brought financial success to the company but who operates outside of the values of the organization. Taking overt action to support or challenge these situations involves the application of physical energy—the leader must be seen **doing** them.

Many programs and processes are key to an organization's success. Leaders need to make difficult choices on how to apply their physical energy to champion the programs most critical to their success. A well-known example of this kind of behavior is Jack Welch's presence in early work-out sessions at General Electric. Work-out is a process with clear purpose and much pre-work. Small groups of managers and employees enabled by pre-session garnering of human and informational resources, address critical business issues, develop recommendations, and present them to the senior leader sponsoring the work. After open dialogue, the leader makes on-the-spot, yes-or-no decisions on those recommendations, empowers people to carry out those that are approved, and afterwards reviews progress to make sure that results are actually achieved. Jack Welch had been nicknamed Neutron Jack because of the firings he championed to reduce the bureaucracy that had built up over the years at GE. Welch knew something needed to be put in the place of the bureaucracy and even the top-down decision making he executed early in his tenure. In fact, Jack Welsh said, "One of the ways we'll know that Work-Out has been successful is that my style of leadership will no longer be tolerated in this company."[8] His visible championing of work-out enabled a process essential to the success of the company.

It takes physical energy and the stamina to withstand physical discomfort for a leader to stay the course in the application of financial resources. An organization's need for financial resources is often analogous to a plant's need for water. When times get tough the financial resources required of key initiatives cannot be withdrawn—this will greatly diminish their likelihood of success. A great example is the importance of maintaining investments in leadership development initiatives when your

---

8.   Ulrich, Dave, Kerr, Steve, and Ashkenas, Ron. *GE-Workout.* New York: McGraw Hill, 2002, p. 3

talent pipeline is core to your future success. All too many companies hamper their near futures by making cost cuts for the supposed benefit of the immediate bottom line. Even stock analysts are beginning to see the correlation between a corporation's investment in the future of its people and the sustainability of that corporation.

Developing and maintaining physical energy requires leaders to care for their own health and well being and to become conscious of the workings and requirements of their own bodies. Each individual is different and needs to develop the means to know what provides them with energy. But it is safe to say that the behind-the-desk, chair sitting, heavy lunch and long hours of yesteryear won't supply the energy our leaders need today and tomorrow. This means leadership development programs, leadership coaching, and individual development plans all need to help our leaders develop strategies for ensuring their busy schedules leave time for things like exercise, restorative family time, meditation, and healthy foods. Like plants, even drinking enough water is important to heightening the energy leaders have available to physically apply back on the job.

INTELLECTUAL ENERGY

Intellectual energy is used by leaders when they are willing and able to apply significant time and thought to deciphering the problems and opportunities facing their organizations. Strategic planning has always been an act that applied intellectual energy, but today's leaders have to be willing to grapple with the greater complexities posed by our truly global economy. Increasingly our threats are also our opportunities and our competitors can also be our partners. This confusing landscape requires mega doses of intellectual energy to effectively resolve into a coherent strategy and business model.

The development of tactical plans has also always required the application of intellectual energy, but today's leaders must be able to hold multiple potential tactics in their thoughts. This multiplicity enables the identification of the best tactics to support the mission, values, strategy, culture, and structure of their organizations under ever changing circumstances. The intellectual energy required for the comparative analysis of tactics has moved far beyond the traditional analysis of three alternative cases. The degree of change in our world today requires space for the evolution of tactical structures while they are being designed and even under implementation so that every tactic could have in reality an unlimited number of permutations. Applying intellectual energy to the appropriate number and combination of alternatives becomes an essential ability for today's leaders.

The holding of multiple time horizons is also a requirement of today's leaders and an application of intellectual energy. Analyzing for both the long- and the short-term requirements of the business, holding what can often appear to be paradoxical perspectives, is essential to organization success. Leaders cannot allow the future or the present to be hostages to each other, and they must both remember and forget components of their organizations' pasts in order to effectively move forward. What to remember, what to forget, whether it is essential in any particular decision to accent the long or the short term or do the best you can for both is an intellectual act that is guided by an intellectual discipline to keep the mind ever focused on the organization's mission.

The development of strategy and tactics and the balancing of the long- and short-term requirements of the business have become more complex and require greater intellectual energy then they did in the first three waves of the economy discussed earlier. But there are many new endeavors requiring the intellectual energy of the leader that did not exist much before the 1990s and are now, in the Fourth Wave economy, still only at the forefront of their eventual importance to business success. I refer to the need to develop and engage with cutting-edge approaches and seek out multiple forms of innovation. The fast pace of business today means that our products and therefore our processes must be innovated continuously. Again leaders must be willing and able to apply the intellectual discipline to search out these innovations in the light of the mission of their specific organizations without falling victim to another company's innovation. We saw this often with reengineering and even work-out when applied to an inappropriate culture or vision.

Many actions by leaders require more than one form of energy. Today the requirement of influencing others involves the application of both intellectual and emotional energies. Influence has always been part of the business world, but the presence of influencing within a network without authority or perhaps even without differentiating levels of expertise as a source of influence, is recent. Influencing a network requires much more thought—intellectual energy to consider how to reach the people you need to influence, who to go to first, who operates as a hub that can make communication more efficient to an exponential degree.

All leaders today are change agents. The degree of change in our world and the innovation required to meet it demands this skill in our leaders. The role of change agent requires enormous applications of intellectual energy. Change agents continually need to consider when to intervene and when to let go. They need to plan for the information and support requirements of a broad array of constituencies and know when they can effectively influence.

There are many leadership actions requiring intellectual energy. How do we foster this energy in our leaders? We need to create oases in which they can practice. We need to tax their minds with metaphors and simulations that they can readily apply later on the job. We need to help with the synthesizing of data so that it can become information, and information can become knowledge, and knowledge eventually wisdom.

Our coaching, leadership development programs, and ordinary leadership team meetings need to enable these development opportunities.

EMOTIONAL ENERGY

Emotional energy is demonstrated by the willingness and abilities of leaders to authentically display a passion about the organization's mission and his or her role in it. To do this they must be able to use tone of voice, gestures, and other communication skills to demonstrate their commitment and belief in the organization's mission, vision, and values. This enables their organization to *know* what is most important at each moment in the organization's life. Emotional energy, combined with intellectual energy, leads in the application of intuition. Intuition has become an increasingly necessary leadership competence as ever-changing business circumstances require fast paced and yet grounded decision making. The ability to

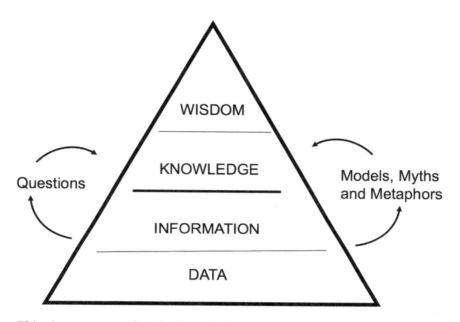

This view suggests that the knowledge worker's task is to generate enough perspective to lift her view above the masses of readily available data and information.

retain emotional memories of characteristics of similar situations that were resolved successfully and apply them in a circumstance with similar characteristics is a key form of leadership intuition required today.

Emotions have not easily found a home in today's work environments. Emotion can even be an uncomfortable domain of conversation for some leaders. So how do we develop emotional energy in our leaders? By creating opportunities for leaders to witness and be coached in the effective communication of their critical messages. By offering intellectual support for the effectiveness of emotional content. By providing analogies to historic speeches of great leaders from Kennedy to Gandhi. By providing places where our leaders can tell the stories of their own emotions without fear and process their emotional, physical, and intellectual energies into the best way they can personally and authentically message to their organizations.

MEANINGFUL ENERGY

Meaningful energy describes the leader's capacity to source energy and emanate energy to inspire and engage others. There is a great hunger today for meaning making. Leaders who can help make meaning for the members of their organizations ensure alignment with the mission and greater energy within the organization. This requires making connections from within the organization to the community in which it operates and to the broader world beyond. When everyone, each and every "Unit of One," (Part II, Chapter 2) see their place in the organization and its mission, energy abounds. Storytelling is key to the ability to make meaning. Providing opportunities for our leaders to develop this skill is essential.

Perhaps it is true that leadership is getting harder, but there may be a different interpretation: one born out of this view of energy enveloping more and more leaders. We no longer exist in a command-and-control structure. There are more and more people who need to function in roles that we would all recognize as roles of leadership. When we recognize this, when we live this, when we each bring forth our emotional, intellectual, physical, and meaningful energy, the burden of leadership is eased. When we move it from the shoulders of the few to the hearts and arms of the many the burden is eased. The gift of combining the generations in our leadership mix, enabling generations Y and Z to lead with X and the Baby Boomers, is to finally and completely recognize the capacity of our global family to develop leadership in each and every "Unit of One"[9] so that all of the generative leadership of the world can emerge.

---

9. "Unit of One," is a term coined by *Fast Company* magazine in the 1990s to refer to "going beyond the old economy where business revolved around the organization — to a new economy where the organization revolves around the individual." http://www.fastcompany.com/magazine/05/edpage5.html

THE NEW WORK OF MANAGEMENT

By Peter Henschel[10]

Executive Director Emeritus
Institute for Research on Learning

In our enterprises today, the search for talent is everything. It is all about recruiting, orienting, socializing, retaining, and renewing commitment and the social contract between employer and employee.

Whether in boom or bust times, recruiting and retaining the very best talent is bedrock critical. A robust economy only makes the challenge more competitive. But the challenge never goes away, no matter what shape the economy or a specific market is in at any given time.

The intellectual capital, knowledge, wisdom, and loyalty that employees choose to bring with them to work make or break companies today. The consequences of poor human capital policies are often swift and unforgiving.

Managers have no greater task than to support and nurture the development of human capital—and that means giving people what they need to succeed.

---

10. Peter Henschel passed away in 2002. Mr. Henschel agreed to include this article in this InterClass book but sadly did not live to see its publication or complete an updated revision himself. We felt it inappropriate to edit posthumously Peter's insightful and still timely article.

New, exciting technologies now drive the methods and speed of everything. We need to be ever more mindful that constantly improving innovation, performance, and productivity comes down to people and what they know, what they share, what they have learned, and what they choose to do with what they know.

And the key to gaining people's loyalty, trust, focus, priorities, engagement, and commitment comes from culture, values, and beliefs, plus management and leadership practices. In order to increase the productivity and effectiveness of employees, we need to develop strong emotional connections between employees and the enterprise...from the first day on the job.

The constant realities in the everyday life of all our enterprises require us to redesign our employee orientation and management development programs. Most enterprises try to make them better, and we also constantly seem to be gearing up for yet another launch or the need to communicate a new strategy to our employees. Yet these tasks often rely far too much on deeply engrained training and communications practices that long ago lost their luster or their power to inspire.

Study after study tells us that people choose to leave an enterprise because they could no longer tolerate their immediate manager. Often, that manager never understood that a major part of their role was to facilitate learning, knowledge sharing, knowledge creation, and continual innovation across the organization—all integral to weaving the fabric of emotional connection and continuous learning.

Assuming compensation is fair (or close), what most employees want is a positive answer to these questions: "Can I grow here? Will I be able to learn what I need to know to be effective and competitive? Will I be able to learn all the time, any time, everywhere while I am engaged in the work of this company? Am I encouraged to learn from others? If I share what I know, will others share with me?"

It all comes down to learning, an organization's ecology, and the supports in place for continuous learning in work.

While recruitment and retention are the visible critical tasks, building continuous, pervasive, everywhere, all the time learning into work practices is the key new challenge for healthy enterprises. Integrating learning seamlessly into work practices is less visible, less understood, and less spoken about. Nonetheless, it is the foundation for all we do to support and nurture the human capital that people bring to their work in order to remain engaged and committed. Doing this well, day by day, adds strategic and tactical value all along the journey.

Was It Not Ever Thus?

In these crazy, on-the-edge times of accelerating change and unnerving uncertainty, it is not enough to rely on "empowered high-performance work teams" to succeed. Nor do the buzzwords and platitudes around "knowledge management" and "empowerment" give us much insight. The new realities demand a deep understanding and belief in the ways people actually and naturally learn, and to act based on that understanding, day by day.

Bottom line: The manager's core work in this new economy is to create and support a work environment that nurtures continuous learning. Doing this well moves us closer to having an advantage in the never-ending search for talent.

Even if this was ever the case, our organizations rarely give this need for continuous learning the attention it deserves. Now, more than ever before, it's an imperative, and will be so for the duration.

I lay out below some of the principles that I believe should influence managers and leaders as they explore their new roles and responsibilities in the new economy. I believe these principles can help us breed the innovation, loyalty, trust, and unbridled creativity that will make all the difference in our competitive world. I originally wrote parts of this essay as a contribution for Jim Botkin's 1999 book, *Smart Business*. With the never-ending competition for talent firmly in mind, I decided to revisit the issues I raised in that essay and want to share with you expanded and updated reflections based on nearly three years of additional practice and observation.

By sheer force of habit, we often substitute training for real learning. Managers often think training leads to learning or, worse, that training *is* learning. But people do not really learn with classroom models of training that happen episodically. These models are only part of the picture. Asking for more training is definitely not enough—it isn't even close. Seeing the answer as "more training" often obscures what's really needed: lifelong, continuous learning *in* work and *at* work.

The Institute for Research on Learning (IRL)[11] has focused on the research and design of learning, in all its facets, to create effective learning. IRL has done this work in a highly iterative participatory design approach with myriad partners, both for K–12 schools and for the world of work. In the area of workplace learning—my focus here—this work has been conducted in a deeply collaborative and interactive model for research and design with lots of partners and customers, mostly from the corporate world. Those partners have included Xerox, Hughes, Hewlett-Packard, Sun Microsystems, Zurich Financial, State Farm Insurance, Nynex, Motorola, and Steelcase, among others. Out of all IRL's projects, a set of enduring principles of learning evolved that have been consistently recognized as important.

From Apprenticeship to "Communities of Practice"

Shortly after IRL's founding in 1987 by a generous multiyear grant from the Xerox Foundation, IRL began to closely examine various models of apprenticeship. IRL discovered that apprenticeship is actually quite widespread, is usually deemed to be successful, and—very importantly— usually works because it requires becoming a member of a cohesive, informal community that goes beyond one master or mentor. Wanting to become "one of them," to be accepted into a community, is a powerful dynamic of apprenticeship. Further, we came to understand that newcomers learn best as they become members of these communities. Moreover, they continue to learn as they, in turn, teach, mentor, and participate "in the practice." Continuing to learn, we discovered, is an equally powerful prerequisite for continuing membership in those communities.

Out of that early work, IRL researchers, beginning with Etienne

11. The Institute for Research on Learning (IRL) is a highly respected Silicon Valley-based international interdisciplinary R&D learning research and design center that merged its operations into San Francisco-based WestEd in April 2000.

Wenger and Jean Lave, developed a term and concept, "Communities of Practice," that has now gained recognition and encouraging acceptance in the learning literature. The Institute is proud to have coined the term, to see it spread, and to work with myriad partners on practical applications of the concept.

Communities of practice are simply those highly informal groups of people who develop a shared way of working together to accomplish some activity. Usually, such communities include people with varying roles and experience. Every organization has them. They don't appear on the "org charts," but this largely invisible informal but cohesive network of people get the real work done. They are also the place where people tend to learn the essentials of their job—just as apprentices do—by participating in them. One might even say that a community of practice is like a super apprenticeship system that continually feeds even the most knowledgeable members the new ideas and feedback critical to continuous lifelong learning.

What an organization knows is what's embedded in and among its communities of practice. Recently, much has been made in the business literature of statements like "if company X only knew what it knows," referring to the difficulty of capturing what many individuals know. We have come to understand that much of what any of us knows is "tacit knowledge" embedded in the practices we share with others. So, if we want to know what our organization knows, we should start by identifying our communities of practice and see them as the wellspring of what the organization *really knows*.

That is one reason why preserving the integrity of these informal communities is so important. The worst effects of downsizing and reengineering come from their complete disregard for communities of practice. The fact that training deals only with explicit knowledge, while the value is often in tacit knowledge, is another reason training can get at only part of what is understood to be effective. The other main limitation of traditional classroom training is that it is episodic and mostly relies on "push" (we want you to know this now) rather than "pull" (I need to know this now and am ready to learn it).

Another dimension to the community idea is seldom discussed, but critically important: Learning is powerfully driven by the critical link between learning and identity. **We most often learn with and through others.**

What we choose to learn depends on:

- who we are
- who we want to become
- which communities we wish to join or remain part of.

So, *not* wanting to be like "them" can be enough to keep someone from learning. That fact seems to hold whether we are talking about company apprentices, high school gangs, or seasoned software engineers.

But it gets even more interesting: IRL studies, among others, have shown that as much as 70% of all organizational learning is informal. Every day, informal learning is constant and everywhere. If this insight is true even in a bare majority of enterprises, why would we leave so much learning to sheer chance?

If those social dimensions of learning are as powerful and enduring as they appear to be—and much work (by IRL and others) strongly supports such a contention—then this is important news for organizations. Most organizations implicitly know they need to be continuously innovative through continuous learning. However, again, typical instructor-led classroom training alone does not even come close to addressing the challenge.

Seven Principles of Learning

From extensive fieldwork, IRL developed seven Principles of Learning that provide important guideposts for organizations. These are not "Tablets from Moses." They are evolving as a work in progress. However, it is already clear that they have broad application in countless settings. Think of them in relation to your own experience.

1. **Learning is fundamentally social.** While learning is about the process of acquiring knowledge, it actually encompasses a lot more. Successful learning is often socially constructed and can require slight changes in one's identity, which make the process both challenging and powerful.

2. **Knowledge is integrated in the life of communities.** When we develop and share values, perspectives, and ways of doing things, we create a *community of practice.*

3. **Learning is an act of participation.** The motivation to learn is the desire to participate in a community of practice, to become and remain a member. This is a key dynamic that helps explain the power of apprenticeship and the attendant tools of mentoring and peer coaching.

4. **Knowing depends on engagement in practice.** We often glean knowledge from observation of, and participation in, many different situations and activities. The depth of our knowing depends, in turn, on the depth of our engagement.

5. **Engagement is inseparable from empowerment.** We perceive our identities in terms of our ability to contribute and to affect the life of communities in which we are or want to be a part.

6. **Failure to learn is often the result of exclusion from participation.** Learning requires access and the opportunity to contribute.

7. **We are all natural lifelong learners.** All of us, no exceptions. Learning is a natural part of being human. We all learn what enables us to participate in the communities of practice of which we wish to be a part.

As an IRL trustee, Paul Allaire, chairman of Xerox, once said, "To do things differently, we need to see things differently." As managers think about what to do differently, it helps to appropriate some new eyeglasses and see through the new lenses that the above principles provide. The challenge for each of us is to put on these new eyeglasses and look through them at the realities we face every day.

Communities of Practice, In Practice

Some examples in practice that IRL team members have observed:

- These principles help us understand why kids on a street corner can learn to run all the complex aspects of an illegal drug business but, somehow, cannot learn math in school. Their identity is wrapped up in the first venture; their engagement absent from the latter.

- The seven principles also help us understand why co-location alone does not necessarily help a software team "cohere" and learn together. If its members have not developed a community out of which a new practice develops, no amount of physical or organizational rearranging will make a difference.

- When a new technology requires both sales and service teams to learn "the new stuff" well and faster, it may not be enough to gain the knowledge; it may also require a change or shift in professional identity in order to succeed with customers or other technicians.

- When a well-designed business process or a new system fails in its implementation, it may be because developing new practices, based upon a whole community's understanding of the old ones and its limitations, was not part of the strategy.

All these examples make clear that **training is not equal to learning**. These examples also show that learning does not always go in stages, especially when we are exposed to rich environments in real-life situations. Also, simply specifying skills or competencies does not usually provide what people really need to know—and learn—even if they are placed in the right environment. The principles also help us understand that much of what we often see as "low-level" work is not as routine or as low-level as it may seem. There are essential connections being built, strengthened, and honed among different members of the informal work community.

Leveraging Communities of Practice: The Manager's New Core Work

What does all this mean for those who are in positions of coaching, shaping, managing, and leading in the world of our new economy?

- The new work of managers and leaders is all about creating the enabling conditions for continuous learning, best done by supporting the informal communities in which it most effectively happens. That requires less control, more listening, more facilitation, more brokering and linking of resources and people to one another. It also demands support for policies and practices that—without the benefit of seeing through the fresh lenses of the seven principles—may not appear to be "efficient" or cost justified.

To accomplish the above, managers will also need to shift their focus, perhaps changing their own identities as well. The shift needs to be:

- from teaching and training to coaching, mentoring, brokering, and ultimately continuous learning
- from selling only products to learning from customers
- from an infatuation with building innovative pilot projects— which seldom cross community boundaries—to building on existing pockets of innovation with explicit support to expand and spread what's already working
- from "delivery" as the operative term to natural "construction" and "spread" of ideas and innovations.

It all boils down to some eternal truths, which many of our corporations and other enterprises need to remember or to learn for the first time:

- Listening, observing, and understanding that existing practices and informal communities—and a tenacious commitment to engage—is a prerequisite to effective management, and the management and nurturing of change.
- Thinking of the whole environment in which learning needs to take place—the culture and the facilities, as well as the professional and intellectual aspects—as we design and enable continuous learning.
- Facilitating greater, richer opportunities for those with whom we work. It is necessary to learn through the communities that already exist. Learning across communities and from one another requires special support and deep understanding.
- Supporting every opportunity for learning—and honoring the power of informal learning—is absolutely essential.

- Taking risks, making mistakes, and quickly and routinely learning from them. Remember the eternal truth of healthy organizations: "It is far better to seek forgiveness than to ask for permission." Also, to quote David Kelley, founder of the Palo Alto award-winning design firm, IDEO: "Fail early in order to succeed sooner."

Making these habits of mind and of practice part of organizational culture is key to building and sustaining a healthy learning organization.

What Do We Do Differently on Monday?

Enterprises that understand these principles rely on the power of informal learning as well as the reality of formal learning, through a rich blend of techniques.

The challenge for our leaders today is to exquisitely craft and support a hybrid/blended learning strategy. It needs to seamlessly integrate instructor-led training, e-learning, peer mentoring, peer coaching, games, storytelling, learning maps, and simulations, intensive interactivity, relationship building, and community building. It can then convey an organization's history, context, culture, values, beliefs, and challenges in addition to creating the learning foundation for all that will come to be learned day by day. With the same rich hybrid blend of learning tools, we can create the transparency and authenticity needed for employees to emotionally tie themselves to the enterprise and what it represents. When this is done well, knowledge acquisition, knowledge sharing, knowledge creation, and continuous innovation cannot be far behind.

For example: Storytelling. One of the values of exemplary corporate learning strategies today lies in its reliance on the power of storytelling to create authenticity and powerful connectedness to the company early on. Through a multi-media experience that shares stories, told by a wide range of diverse employees, a story unfolds that engages rather than simply "tells." The best examples build connectedness to the organization early through the power of multi-media and then use hands-on discovery oriented interactive team-building techniques to create and sustain engagement and commitment. This approach creates high retention and commitment through a learning perspective that relies, again, on the "pull" (need, want, desire) from the learner, versus a "push" (should have now, deliver, force feed) from the instructor. This approach to telling the story of a company—its history, business context, values, beliefs, and aspirations—helps new recruits see the company through the deeply human eyes of the people who ARE the company. Through these powerful messages and images, the learner comes to develop an understanding of the key insights with others, gaining a shared context and transparency early and maintaining that approach throughout the learning journey.

A number of companies, such as Charles Schwab, Levi Strauss, and Sun Microsystems with the help of learning firms such as San Francisco-based Design Media, Inc. are making authentic story-telling an integral part of their learning strategies, especially for orientation when the challenge of gaining commitment and emotional connection is greatest. Other companies, including Xerox, State Farm, Zurich Financial Services and Motorola have embraced the IRL Learning Principles in their learning strategies, with the initial help of IRL and now with the help of an IRL professional services firm spin off, the Strategic Practices Group, also based in San Francisco.

After the first orientation sessions, we cannot rely on great learning events in the classroom or on the computer screen. Activities such as tours, check-in meetings, informal lunches, and peer coaching are integrated into an "after burn" strategy that keeps the learning ongoing, centered, and growing. As a result, new relationships develop and communities of practice are nurtured as new members join in a cognitive apprenticeship model.

These principles, tools, techniques, and their implications are essential foundations. They help all of us cope, survive, grow, and thrive in this exciting, brave, and scary world of the new economy.

If we do not pay attention to this new management work—and what it demands of us—we face the reality expressed by Intel's CEO, Andy Grove: "There is at least one point in the history of any company when you have to change dramatically to rise to the next performance level. Miss the moment, and you start to decline."

Peter Henschel

Peter Henschel at the time of his passing was chief learning officer of the stupski family foundation and executive director emeritus of the Institute for Research on Learning (whose operations are now mostly part of San Francisco-based WestEd). He served as a retained advisor and consultant for companies building or renewing corporate universities and learning programs, both adult and K–12, and eLearning companies. He was a frequent national and international speaker on issues of learning, management development, innovation, human capital, and organizational health.

The author expressed his gratitude for all of the work and insights of IRL and its people that informed his perspective in this essay.

A TIME FOR TRANSCENDENT LEADERSHIP

By Carlos Mota Margain

"Everything has changed but our thinking"
~ Albert Einstein ~

My intention in this chapter is to analyze the underlying paradigm on which today's management theory and practice are rooted and offer a new and wider approach to go about creating the necessary conditions to help our organizations adopt a new and emergent paradigm.

In essence, my hypothesis is that the world has changed dramatically and that instead of making efforts to understand the nature of this accelerating change, we are holding on to old practices and approaches. We are doing it without realizing that it is not incremental improvements that will help us face existing and future challenges but, for the first time in several centuries, current context that calls for a true evolution of leadership that can help us find new ways to create sustainable and human centered success and well being for people, organizations.

The ozone hole in organizations

As globalization evolves into a worldwide phenomenon where no place on earth seems to escape from its influence, there is a growing gap between the ever increasing demand on corporations to grow faster and more profitably and the organizational capacity to deliver these results over time.

The market, competition, and Wall Street are the main pressures that raise these demands. Firms in today's world need to fulfill these demands or face the consequences of being replaced by others that perform accordingly.

However, many organizations seem to fail in responding to the complex nature and accelerating changes in the environment. This situation creates a gap between the required performance in organizations and the effectiveness of their responses. This gap creates a substantial pressure on leaders to better attract and manage available resources.

As this gap widens, leaders turn to academia, gurus, consultants, and other external sources for help. In most cases, these sources are not only expensive but also addictive in the sense that, as the world grows in complexity and uncertainty, there is a greater dependency on them. In many cases, the help comes in the form of new tools that create a short-term relief of the gap but after a while, the gap grows again and, often, the intervention creates unanticipated negative effects in the organization.

Perhaps the most important unintended consequence of many organizational practices and interventions is the dehumanization of work. The current addiction to external solutions mainly oriented to design efficient systems, processes, or technological applications, is making organizations and mainly the individual pay an extremely high price. The price is paid in terms of stress and physical weariness as well as reduced passion, conviction, and sense of meaning of life.

Like the hole in the ozone layer of the atmosphere, we are witnessing a growing void in the layer of human spirit in the organization's atmosphere that limits and restrains human potential.

The effect of this is the fragmentation of the doing and the being in individuals as well as in the organization as a whole.

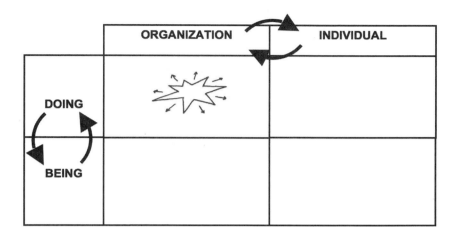

The center of the attention in organizations has been almost exclusively its performance (doing), relegating the being, therefore creating an important imbalance.

Challenging an objectivist view of life

A key element that helps us understand current reality is the underlying paradigm present in human practices in every domain that has been strengthened over the last century.

The term "paradigm" was popularized by Thomas Kuhn in *The Structure of Scientific Revolutions*, as a model of society with which most people concur. He defines paradigm as "...a constellation of concepts, values, perceptions and practices shared by a community which forms a particular vision of reality that is the basis of the way a community organizes itself."

Individuals have mindsets or mental models, while entire communities share a paradigm—the basic operating assumptions that hold the social system together.

As it has been stated by many authors in recent years, we are still living under a Cartesian/Newtonian worldview, where organizations are conceived through a mechanistic, cause-effect, and linear thinking.

We might call this an objectivist worldview since it sees reality as an array of "objects" that require manipulation to produce desired results and to fix any deviations toward its goals. We might also call this worldview cybernetic in the sense that it is focused on controlling the performance of the organization on a given pattern. Cybernetics implies a negative feedback loop with three distinct phases: a) discover a deviation from a predetermined performance, b) choose an offsetting action, and c) carry out the offsetting action and back again to the first phase. This cybernetic approach is, in essence, an application of the engineer's idea of control applied to human activity.

A simple but clear way to understand this paradigm is the familiar figure of input >> process >> output.

Current thinking is based on the following premise: If I want a specific pre-determined result (output), then my task is to design an effective way to combine and use the minimum amount of resources possible in an efficient process to produce the desired outcome. Once the process

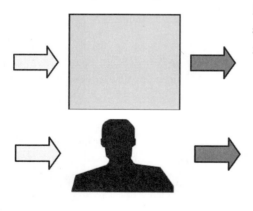

is underway, my job will be to adjust and fine tune the performance of the system.

This way of looking has, in my opinion, a major flaw. When looking at the world through the lens of existing paradigm, we see things, people and life as objects susceptible to control, manipulation, and use. Following this line of thought, basically they all are resources. We changed the name of nature calling it natural resources and people to human resources. This is not a trivial semantic problem. It is more profound than that. When thinking of them as resources, we give ourselves permission to utilize them for the sake of results, mainly in the form of profits or economic gain.

In the case of managing people, our task has been to decide which inputs will trigger the necessary internal processes in the individual so that he or she develops the needed attitude, action, or performance. Some of the theories behind this paradigm are behavioral psychology, reduction-ism, and humanistic psychology.

A metaphor of leadership in the existing paradigm: The rowing boat

One of the most challenging problems in organizations is how to best coordinate the human effort in order to produce the desired outcome. The industrial revolution required a new form of organizing people in the factories to ensure an efficient productive process. This was the birth of the familiar pyramidal organizational chart concept, where the factory was divided into functions and specialties and activities were organized in job positions with clear-cut limits and where command and control was the name of the game. Although we have made some minor modifications, this approach still prevails in our times.

A metaphor that captures the role of leaders and followers under this paradigm is a rowing boat.[12] This is a very efficient vessel, slim and long, designed to cruise at high speeds. It has a visible leader and followers face him or her with their backs to the future, waiting for orders to be implemented. Obedience, strength, perfect coordination, and standard-ization are essential for this boat to perform effectively.

This is an extremely effective design for still waters and for a straight line trajectory. Unfortunately, there are all kinds of indications that tell us that the waters in which organizations sail today are not still. It

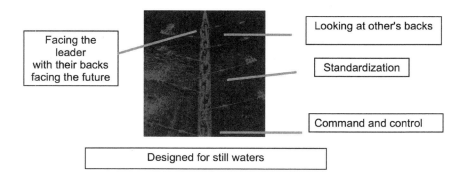

Facing the leader with their backs facing the future

Looking at other's backs

Standardization

Command and control

Designed for still waters

---

12. In the context of this article, "rowing boat" refers to a racing skull or crew boat, rather than a "row boat" with a single rower, as in common American usage.

appears that we are in troubled waters. The effects of this metaphor when facing white waters are significant.

Impact of the rowing metaphor in turbulent organizational waters	
EFFECTS ON THE BEING	EFFECTS ON THE DOING
• The being is subordinated to the doing • People feel alienated as they are treated as resources • Diminishing sense of passion, energy, and commitment • Lack of sense of meaning of life in the organization—"life happens outside" • Underdeveloped human potential	• Reducing ability to foresee and control • Increasing anxiety, fear of failure, and hostility toward the organization • Seeking recipes that produce successful outcomes, and when they fail, they jump to the next "savior recipe" • Reduced internal capacity in organizations to deliver the ever growing demands for results

Leadership at a crossroads

Perhaps it is possible now to better understand the great pressure that most leaders in organizations face today. On the one hand there is a top down pressure to deliver better and faster results every day. On the other hand, there is a pressure from employees in the lower layers of the structure to be heard and taken into account as integral human beings and not just as resources to produce desired output. Finally, they, as human being themselves, feel the anxiety, uncertainty, and, in many cases, frustration and helplessness that cannot be expressed freely because it might not be considered appropriate behavior—according to current thinking—coming from a leader.

Leaders today, when facing these pressures, ask insistently how to apply new methodologies and what new behaviors they can adopt immediately. As Ralph Stacey would state in his *Complexity and Creativity in Organizations*, the fundamental question asked by leaders under the current paradigm is, how can we design our organizations so that they will yield successful outcomes?

I believe that such a question, which under current thinking would look so natural and familiar, leads us and leads our leaders into a vicious circle in a never ending search for "savior" recipes or "flavor of the month."

As these sources provide just temporary relief to the fundamental needs of the organization, leaders continue to be on the spot and at the center of what has been called today a crisis of leadership.

I believe that orientation to results at any rate is back firing in the way of diminished use and development of the organization's capacities such as creativity and innovation, strategic alertness, and agility, among other undesired consequences. My belief is that it is not only convenient or necessary to be aware of the fragmentation of the being and the doing, it is crucial to understand it and to imagine new harmonic ways to allow individuals to be fully present in the organization. To stop thinking that life happens after work and, look at myself and my work as important parts of me. As a top executive in Pfizer Spain once told me: "my work is my life...too!" For this to happen, it would be necessary to realize that people are not resources and to believe, in our minds and hearts, that we can create conditions for a win-win proposition: the health, growth, and profitability of our organization and, at the same time and as an integral part of this dynamic, create the conditions for individuals to tap, liberate and manifest the best of what they are, and to set free their full potential as human beings. By doing so, groups and teams will become alive, energized, with an authentic sense of belonging and strong intentions that can be translated into commitments and accountability at work and in life.

The good news is that, contrary to the case of the ozone hole, the hole in human spirit in organizations is reversible. We—human beings—have the capacity and power to reverse it, as we once had the capacity and power that created it.

The emergence of a different paradigm

A new and entirely different pattern of thought is beginning to emerge worldwide and in various fields of human activity, driven by a fresh set of conditions and challenges. The new paradigm is beginning to find expression in the natural and the social sciences, especially in education and philosophy. This new paradigm is being shaped by contributions from academic and scientific disciplines. Insights from quantum physics, and complexity and chaos theory are being applied in understanding the functioning of the brain, social behavior, stock-market cycles, and weather patterns.

Traditionalists are being challenged by a new generation of integrative and open systems thinkers. New disciplines are emerging in psychology, ecological evolution, general systems theories, and others. Everything is being called into question. The sacred cows are no longer safe.

This emerging paradigm must help leaders to deal with complexities, uncertainty, and accelerating change greater than what is present now and throughout our planet's turbulent history. A new paradigm could be weak or sterile if it is not driven by ethical principles and values. The new emergent paradigm calls not only for adequate responses and understanding of the environment and its changes, it calls us and leaders to rescue the human spirit of the organization, to create working spaces where people and the organization as a whole can be successful without losing their soul. Therefore, I believe that this new emergent paradigm has a strong human content that can allow us to develop a different worldview. This is, as Marcel Proust suggests:

"The true voyage of discovery
Consists not in going to unknown landscapes,
But in having new eyes"

Essentially the new paradigm requires that we develop new eyes, that we can see (think and feel) differently. I believe this is the calling of our times. This is the calling in the phrase of Albert Einstein in the opening of this chapter. This is the calling of human kind.

Some of the principles of the new paradigm are:

- There is goodness in life and in human beings.
- Life is based on diversity. Diversity of ideas and individuals is

a source of richness.

- Each individual is co-creator of reality.
- We need to treat each person as expert in something and nobody as the expert in everything.
- Learning is an essential driver for evolution.
- Knowledge is created through non-conventional practices and methods.
- Self-organization is the core process of life.
- Everything is interconnected in dynamic systemic structures.
- Collaboration is essential. Networks of communities of practice is a natural way to work and collaborate.
- Curiosity is more important than certainty.
- Imagination is more important than knowledge.

A new metaphor: Rafting

Imagine a rowing boat trying to cruise in the middle of white waters. What would you think of it? Perhaps that it is absurd, foolish, and a call for disaster. I think that what this situation describes is what we are doing in organizations, institutions, academia, and in almost every realm of human activity. We are holding on to old practices and methods without challenging them. Following our metaphor, it is as if we were trying to "modernize" the rowing boat by providing the crew with a boat made of platinum, computer screens, and a system of satellite communication that provides instant orders and information.

The point I am trying to make is that we are not challenging the design of the boat and the way we need to coordinate ourselves to face turbulent uncharted waters.

Some years ago, a good friend and visionary man, Willis Harman, asked me, "Carlos, what is our next metaphor?" I have to admit that at that moment I did not understand Willis' question. After about ten years the question still resonates in me. An attempt to answer this profound inquiry is the idea of rafting. A rafting boat and its crew suggest many ideas that might prove appropriate for human coordination in times that have been defined by several authors as being at the edge of chaos, or as Dee Hock's term "chaordic," suggests, moving constantly from chaos into order and into chaos again.

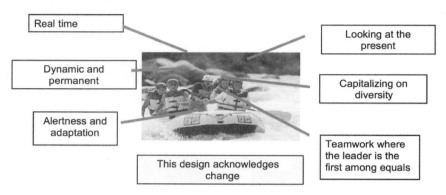

This metaphor invites us to reconsider traditional approaches to human coordination and to challenge the industrial age idea of leadership still pervasive in our days.

The use and assimilation of this metaphor could have a very positive impact both on the being and on the doing in organizations.

Impact of the rafting metaphor in turbulent organizational waters	
EFFECTS ON THE BEING	EFFECTS ON THE DOING
• The being and the doing act in harmony and reinforce each other	• Acting with more confidence under uncertainty
• People have the freedom and joy of being themselves and to contribute to the best of their capacities	• Promote self-control
	• Sense of thrill facing risk with poise and determination
• Tremendous energy, passion, and commitment	• Continuously experimenting with new approaches in synonymy with the context realizing that there is not a single right answer
• Clear inner sense of meaning of the journey—"I am fully alive in this ride"	• Strengthened inner capacity of the team to successfully face turbulent times and be prepared/anticipate what might come next
• Unleashed human potential of each individual	

Integrating the Doing and the Being

Over the last ten years I have been experimenting with the incorporation of this emerging paradigm into daily work and life in organizations. These applications have included functional areas like general management, planning, human resources, marketing and operations in all levels of the organizational structure.

During this time I have witnessed a transition in the attitude of managers from confusion and resistance to these ideas, to initial interest and opening to listen more and to experiment. Curiosity to me is the initial step in a voyage of discovery. This curiosity can allow leaders to make deliberate efforts to understand, assimilate, and practice a new-paradigm approach to himself, to people, and to the business.

In doing so, he or she can discover new ways to integrate the doing and the being both of individuals and the organization, instead of concentrating all efforts in just one area: the performance of the business as it suggests in the current paradigm. An integrative approach can be depicted as a spiral that expands as the leader and the organization continue engaging an integrative dynamic.

The Integrative Spiral

This integrative approach starts with a focus on organizational performance but also incorporates the need to strengthen the doing of the individual. Additionally this spiral embodies what has been named as the "soft" side of the organization: the being of the individual person and

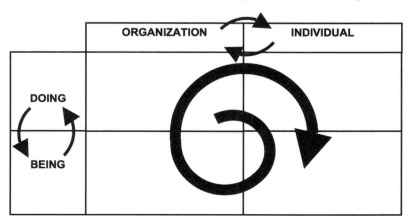

the collective being of teams and the organization. The premise depicted here is as follows: only when individuals and groups are fully integrated—in their doing and being—can they perform and deliver extraordinary results and excel in every aspect of their lives with freewill and conviction. In contrast, limited or fragmented individuals and groups can only deliver when facing external force, control, or incentives.

The new task of the leader

Move beyond achievements toward Transcendence

One of the key changes in new-paradigm leaders is the reconsideration of results. A new leader must switch from the consideration of achievements as the final goal of himself/herself or the organization, to the realization that results and achievements are the necessary means to move in the direction of the higher human and organizational aspirations, that is a sense of transcendent purpose.

This does not reduce the importance of results. It only puts them in perspective. When we act with clarity about our purpose, then our results have meaning. And not only that, if we have a clear purpose, not every result would be in harmony with it. We can discriminate and choose to pursue those achievements that will move us nearer our purpose. Additionally, we can be careful in selecting the processes, systems, and activities that are congruent with our purpose, in line with the claim that the end result does not justify the means to achieve it.

I would like to suggest a third element to complement achievements and purpose: Capabilities. A clear sense of purpose will suggest the kind of capabilities that are needed to generate the required achievements.

This triad of purpose, capabilities, and achievements is a continuum that could guide people and organizations to clarify and integrate:

- the transcendent with the day to day activities
- the doing with the being
- the means with the end goal.

This model requires at its core a set of ethical values and principles that are present in every action and also requires some of the fundamental attributes of human beings. I suggest the following three:

Freedom—This gift of humans that makes us accountable for our acts and responsible to what we do with our acts and life. This is opposed to following blindly external signals.

Consciousness—A higher level of awareness. The perception of the interconnectedness of everything to everything else. A powerful sense of being present in the full meaning of the term. This is opposed to inertia and shallow sight of things.

Will—The courage and determination and perseverance to move and act. To use our strength and vigor to face and surpass difficulties in our journey.

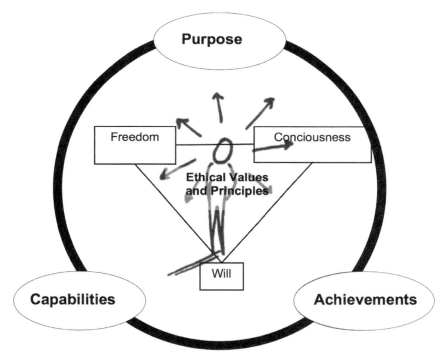

With these elements, we can attempt to create a model that can help leaders to incorporate a transcendent view of their task. To help people and the collective to find ways to see beyond the immediate. To work passionately and with a clear intention. You might remember an old story of a visitor to a construction site asking one of the workers what he was doing. "I am carving stones." As he continued walking the visitor asked another worker, what are you doing? "I am building a cathedral!" This is precisely what this model offers: a new-paradigm leader, the possibility of creating the conditions for people to make sense of life in the organization and to unleash the full range of his/her human capacities. It is urgent to re-discover the true meaning of work and this model invites leaders to adopt some fundamental elements without prescribing a predetermined path as Antonio Machado, the Spanish poet suggests: "Caminante, no hay camino, se hace camino al andar…" (Traveler, there is no road, you create the road as you walk…).

The transition from leader as hero to the adoption of transcendent leadership

In moving from an old-paradigm to a new-paradigm thinking about life and work, you need to approach yourself differently. This entails two fundamental questions that we seldom have the time or courage to identify or face: Who am I? and What do I want in life? This is a truly philosophical question that we need to address because being a new-paradigm leader requires that I start with myself and then think about others, acknowledging that my relationships affect me and that I have an impact on others. It is most important to change our input>process>output schema to a more organic and fluid one. We are social human beings. We can only be conceived in relationship with others. Although we have paid much attention to the individuality of a person, in reality we are formed and influenced by others since the time we are born. However this does not eliminate our freedom. We are free to act according to the influence of others or else especially if we are conscious and have the courage or will to act differently.

I see the individual and the collective not as different entities or beings, but as complementary to each other in a complex, dynamic relationship. The picture I offer is a continuous cycle, similar to a sign of infinity that flows between the person as individual and the collective where both influence the other at the same time and in a permanent fashion. In linear thinking we might be tempted to ask: Who is first? Who is the most important actor? However under the new-paradigm thinking a natural question would be, What is the nature of the process by which the individual and the group influence each other?

The adoption of a transcendent view of leadership is a transformational process that starts with myself and then moves in the relationship with others.

Transformation then can be defined as the inner and voluntary change of individuals and communities of work in the way they perceive themselves and others, generating a clear vision of what they want to be or create in the future (purpose), developing the best of what they are (capabilities) in order to achieve the necessary results (achievements) to advance in the search of our purpose.

From theory to practice

I remember a good friend many years ago telling me that he had attended a great course that followed a specific text book. He said that they didn't finish the book; we got to chapter 10. I borrowed his book and read the title of chapter 11 "From theory to practice." We both laughed realizing that the course ended just before putting everything to the acid test of practice.

I would like to move into the most relevant aspect of this chapter that is voiced by many executives who ask me constantly, How can we incorporate the new paradigm in my workplace? How can we put all of this that sounds relevant in our work? How can we face the resistance that we will encounter within our organizations when trying to apply these concepts?

If you notice, these frequent questions start with a how. Current paradigm is based on the permanent search for the solution, for specific steps to follow, for a clear-cut methodology that ensures success. Unfortunately for many and interestingly for others, the new-paradigm approach cannot provide the solution. It can only offer suggestions, approaches, or stimuli. It is up to us (as individuals and as a group) to find, discover, co-create the how's. Sometimes a title in a book tells a great deal. This is the case of one of the recent books by Peter Block: *The Answer to How is Yes*. Using this phrase, we can say that in order to find the hows of the new paradigm, we first need to say yes to it. Only then can we embark on a journey to co-create the hows every time, understanding that none of them could be the solution to our problems.

Therefore, what I would like to suggest is a series of recommendations based on my consulting practice in Mexico, the U.S., and Europe with the intention to provide some guidance to be better prepared for the journey toward transcendent leadership. In this journey the new-paradigm leader needs to

Develop multiple roles

- **Focalizer**, generating shared vision, mission, position, and attention.
- **Facilitator**, bringing about commitment, action, harmony, and growth.
- **Synergizer**, helping to achieve individual/organizational/ societal congruence.
- **Co-creator**, position oneself as co-learner and co-shaper of success. The first among equals, not the "hero."
- Help his team to establish agreements in fundamentals.

This could be better understood by considering the following phrase of Saint Augustine in the 5th century:

Collaboration
in everything

Freedom in the rest

Agreements in
fundamentals

"In essence; unity
In the rest; freedom
In everything else; charity"

The power of this thought still prevails and is much needed in our times. Transcendent leaders need to co-create with his/her team a set of agreements in fundamental issues. Once established they are not negotiable until the same group decides to modify them. If each member is a steward of these agreements, the level of trust and cohesion of the group will grow substantially.

Coordinate human effort under a network of communities of work

In current times, we need to organize in flexible, permeable open networks of relationships. Teams or groups, whether functional or multi-disciplinary, fixed or created temporarily for a project, need to be a part of a larger net of teams and exchange learnings, information and ideas. Using the same picture derived from the Saint Augustine phrase, we can envision a network as a dynamic interrelationship where the agreements in fundamentals are shared by the network as well as a space of freedom and a spirit of collaboration.

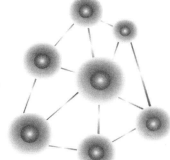

Start an experiment creating a small network of teams that work under new-paradigm thinking

Convene, train, and launch a small group of working teams that start experimenting with a different approach to work. Provide guidance, coaching, and continuous support to generate learning and insights that can be used when expanding the network incorporating other teams.

Distinguish, follow up, and nurture activities in three dimensions

A common problem in today's organizations is the tendency to "fire fighting." It looks like everything is urgent and that we need to stop doing anything else until we finish this pressing task. Once we finish it we have the same need over and over again. Transcendent leaders need to incorporate in their daily agendas and to-do lists the following activities:

- activities that provide short-term visibility and results (working on the imperative)

- activities aimed to address structural issues that will have multiple positive effects (working on leverage points)
- transformational activities whose effects will be visible with time but that need to be initiated now (working on the transcendent).

Promote exceptional results as a result of a generative cycle

It is necessary to understand that sustainable performance in the organization is a natural result of a set of elements, each of which promotes the subsequent:

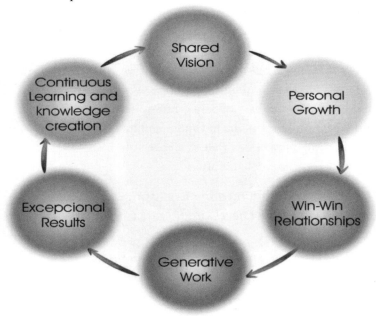

Develop a voluntary educational program on new-paradigm themes and the need for transformation

Some of the capabilities that I suggest be strengthened/developed among team members when starting a transition into transcendent leadership are:

- personal mastery
- systems thinking
- active listening
- being present

- relaxed concentration
- ability to face paradox and ambiguity
- networking and human relationships
- creativity and innovation
- challenging current assumptions and creation of new connections
- convener and facilitator of significant conversations and dialogue
- crisis and conflict management.

Establish an ongoing organizational capability of constant discovery, choice, and action

Transcendent leadership helps create, over time a virtuous cycle in individuals that is incorporated by teams. This cycle consists of the following elements:

Discover—The ability to sense different actors, elements, and events inside and outside the organization as well as their relationships,

Choice—Select a response to those states based on principles and values, agreements in fundamentals and the context discovered in the previous phase,

Act—Translate the previous choice into a reality, acting with courage, will, and determination as well as with integrity.

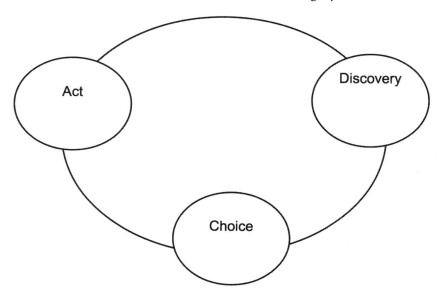

All these suggestions can be a valuable source of ideas to incorporate in the practice of transcendent leadership. I believe that this journey does not have an ending point. It grows and evolves finding new challenges and discovering new ways to face reality in a continuous learning process.

Perhaps it is worth finishing this chapter by posing a question rather than by offering an answer. Since transcendent leadership starts with the person, then let me ask a personal question:

What would it take for me and others to act deliberately and relentlessly in supporting the integration of the being and the doing of individuals and the organization as a whole and to adopt a more transcendent view of work and life?

Carlos Mota Margain

The focus of my work is to support individuals, organizations, and institutions to engage in an evolutionary path that harmonizes their being, doing, and transcending through their work. I call this approach "Transcendent Evolution." It requires that the aim of leadership be transformed from efficiency and productivity at any rate, to achieving the higher purpose of people and organization as a whole. In this article, I describe the type of transcendent leadership that can bring about harmonic change. Since 2004, I have had the privilege of working on several projects with Eric Vogt, Robin Grumman-Vogt, and InterClass, in this exciting journey of learning at a crucial time for humanity.

DESIGNING LEADERS

by Jeanne Liedtka

Executive Director of the Batten Institute for
Entrepreneurship and Innovation and Faculty Member,
Darden School at University of Virginia

Overview: Despite the well-recognized importance of vision to organizational success and change, this author argues that those of us charged with helping leaders to develop have done little to help them build a set of skills critical to visioning—design skills. She describes a new approach that she has worked with that involves using design principles to help leaders understand the substance and principles embedded in effective strategy visioning.

Leadership that matters engages people in designing better futures— for themselves, for their companies, for their countries. We know this. As a result, few aspects of leadership have received more attention than the role of leader as visionary, charged with the prime responsibility for developing their organization's future image and strategic direction. The reasons for this are clear, and have been for a long time. Successful organizations have employees who are *committed*, rather than *compliant*. Engaged employees share their organization's values and are in agreement with what the organization stands for. Absent this, employees trade a day's labor for a day's wage, and this is not what sustains organizational excellence. Today change management capabilities are recognized as key leadership skills.

Thus, the focus on vision and strategy is even more critical. Virtually all change theorists believe a compelling image of the future is fundamental to the ability to accomplish significant change, whether for organizations or individuals.

How has leadership development changed in response to these challenges? In a number of ways, all of which I see as useful, but none of which have proved really adequate to the task at hand. First, we laud "visionary" leaders, telling their stories over and over again in the hope that *observing* the visionary actions of others will enhance one's own visioning skills. Not a bad way to start, but unlikely to significantly enhance the skills of others. After all, most of us seem already able to recognize others' visioning capacity. It's not that we don't know what vision looks like or understand it can produce amazing results; we just don't know how to do it. On the other hand, some of us think we *are* doing it when we're not. So we focus on enhancing leaders' self-awareness of their current visioning skills, using tools like 360-degree feedback and assessment centers. This practice has become widespread in corporations, ones I have worked in included, and virtually every competency model in use today pays prominent attention to a something like "inspiring shared vision." By calling attention to and providing feedback on this dimension of leadership, followed by coaching aimed at improving performance, we hope to help leaders become more visionary. Again, this approach, while valuable, often stops short of building the new competencies needed. An enormous gap may still remain between knowing what you lack and developing it.

The unstated assumption behind both of these approaches is that the ability to create a vision lies within a leader—he or she just needs to pay attention to it. But many of us have wondered whether most executives, by and large, possess an innate capability for visioning. Certainly, their skill sets can be improved through development activities, but many have long suspected that true visionaries are, in fact, usually born rather than made. This renders the prospects for significant improvement in the vision quotient of organizations dim.

Meanwhile, on the other side of the fence, our compatriots toiling in the field of strategy have had a more expeditious approach. Lacking a vision, they just buy one from an expert! While leadership folk tend to see the quality of vision as dependent upon the leader, strategists tend to see it as embedded in the vision itself. Thus, hiring a consultant to help craft a really good vision makes a lot of sense. Unfortunately, in my experience that approach, despite the proliferation of laminated wallet-sized vision cards it has produced, has resulted in even less organizational change, breeding cynicism instead of shared purpose in both leaders and their organizations.

I am an avowed enthusiast of the central role strategic direction plays in creating a company's future. I often come away from executive education experiences intensely frustrated at our inability to move the visioning needle in powerful ways. Despite its enormous significance, the "vision thing" has joined the ranks of so many other over-used management clichés and collapsed under the weight of its own trendiness. Organizations lucky enough to have visionary leaders have vision and the benefits it brings, while the rest of us limp along, deriding the whole "vision thing" as more hot tubs and kumbaya.

Lately, however, I have renewed hope that there is a better way to help develop executives' visioning competency. My inspiration comes from an unlikely place—the world of design.

Why Design?

I began to think in terms of teaching executives design thinking when I picked up Donald Schon's *The Reflective Practitioner: How Professionals Think in Action*.[13] I had gotten very interested in the role of reflection in executive development and found myself re-reading his classic book on learning, which I had read many years before. Once again, the chapter on business managers didn't do much for me. But this time I read the whole book, and the chapter on architecture, with its focus on the design process, blew me away. It reminded me of Nobel Laureate Herb Simon's postulate from the late sixties:

> Engineering, medicine, business, architecture, and
> painting are concerned not with the necessary but with
> the contingent—not with how things are but with how

---

13. D. Schon. The Reflective Practitioner: How Professionals Think in Action. New York: Basic Books, 1983.

they might be—in short, with design… Everyone designs who devises courses of action aimed at changing existing situations into preferred ones… Design, so construed, is the core of all professional training. (Simon, 1969)

As I have come to understand the parallels between the world of design and business practice, what we really mean when we say that successful visions and strategies are designed became much clearer to me. Visions and strategies are created, not discovered. They exist only to the extent that we *will* them into existence. Design fixes our attention directly on *intention* and challenges a leader to conceive of a vision or strategy as focused as the invention of a "purposeful space"—virtual in this case, rather than physical—in which particular activities, capabilities, and relationships are encouraged and a particular kind of community is created. The role of leaders, then, is not just to put some aspirations for the future on paper. Instead, they create a palpable space in which people can *live into* a future that they can see vividly and care about.

Grounding vision creation in the design process creates a different perspective from which to approach improving leaders' skill sets. Even if people are basically already who they are—visionary or not—when we get them; even if the right "answers" still only emerge out of the black box of consultants' tool kits, *processes* can be taught to those who are interested in learning them. Thus, I hypothesized that leaders in organizations, whether visionary or not, can benefit from understanding the processes and skills used by successful designers in fields like architecture, software, and the fine arts. And so I started on my own journey, developing a deeper understanding of the design process and skill set.

Thomas Jefferson: The Design of a Purposeful Space

I started in my own backyard, at the University of Virginia, designed by Thomas Jefferson in the last decade of his life. There is probably no better place to begin to understand the concept of designing a space with a purpose, a space infused by the values of its creator. Jefferson had a lifelong passion for education, which was rooted in the value dearest to him—liberty. He believed that the democracy he so loved, that he and the other founding fathers had succeeded in creating, could only be sustained through the education of the people.

The original portion of the UVA campus that Jefferson designed, the "main grounds," as it is now referred to, remains remarkably unaltered from what Jefferson built in the 1820's. It is widely regarded as one of the most architecturally significant college campuses in the United States today. To the modern observer, Jefferson's genius may appear to lie in the beauty of the buildings that he created. In reality, he took much of his architectural inspiration rather directly from Palladio, a sixteenth-century Italian architect. His true genius lay in the power of the space he created and in its ability to evoke so vividly the purpose for which it was designed. Jefferson said it this way: "the illimitable freedom of the human mind to explore and expose every subject susceptible of its contemplation...For here, we are not afraid to follow truth wherever it may lead, nor to tolerate any error so long as reason is left free to combat it."[14]

Jefferson's University differed from others of its day in many ways—among them, its physical space, its governance policies, and its curriculum. He envisioned an "academical village," a community where faculty and students worked as partners to pursue the kind of learning that democracy required. The typical large central building was replaced with a collection of smaller buildings, grouped together around a common area. As early as 1810, Jefferson had developed a clear image of the early UVA campus:

> I consider the common plan followed in this country, but not in others, of making one large and expensive building, as unfortunately erroneous. It is infinitely better to erect a small and separate lodge for each professor-ship, with only a hall below for his class, and two chambers above for himself; joining these lodges by barracks for a certain portion of the students, opening into a covered way to give a dry communication between all of the schools. The whole of these arranged around an open square of grass and trees, would make it, what it should be in fact, an academical village, instead of a large and common den of noise, of filth, and of fetid air.

---

14. All quotations here are taken from Jefferson's letters—dated 1810 and 1823.

This garden-encircled village was to be a community of learning where students would have unprecedented freedom in both the choice of curriculum and in governing their own behavior: "Our institution will proceed on the principle of doing all the good it can without consulting its own pride or ambition; of letting everyone come and listen to whatever he thinks may improve the condition of his mind," said Jefferson. The curriculum would include the new "scientific" and "pragmatic" fields, like botany and agriculture, as well as classical courses in literature, philosophy, Greek, and Latin. Perhaps most significantly, student self-government would be the principle upon which the new university would run. Thus, Jefferson set out to create a *space* capable of evoking a desired set of behaviors and relationships—which would result in a particular kind of learning. He did not set out to design a set of buildings.

All aspects of UVA's design, from the architecture to the curriculum to the selection of faculty and methods of governance emerged out of an image that Jefferson held of the type of educational *experience* he wanted to create. This image was grounded in the values and beliefs he held most dear—in the promise of democracy and self-government, the power of knowledge and community, the primacy of freedom of choice.

I learned a lot about the design process from Jefferson: the way in which values and purpose, the terrain, the craftsman's capabilities, and a host of other elements are brought together to create a purposeful space, a space that recognizes the power of both form and function, of both the aesthetic and the pragmatic.

Jefferson teaches us that the job of leaders is ultimately to create a space that encourages people to live into some vision of a future they care about. As business leaders, we have a lot of different factors to work with and consider, as Jefferson did. Like his design for UVA, we too must begin with a clear understanding of the institution's values and purpose. Today, when I talk with leaders about vision, I start the conversation with a visit to the University's main grounds, and allow them to experience, first hand, what it feels like to occupy a truly purposeful space.

Frank Gehry: Design as an Iterative Process[15]

I also looked for lessons in leadership from contemporary architects, and found them in the work of perhaps the most famous living architect today—Frank Gehry. In describing the 20th century's 100 "greatest design hits," *New York Times* architecture critic Herbert Muschamp included only one building designed in the last decade, Frank Gehry's Guggenheim Museum in Bilbao, Spain. Writing in the *Los Angeles Times*, Architecture Critic Nicolai Ouroussoff effuses:

> Gehry has achieved what not so long ago seemed impossible for most architects: the invention of radically new architectural forms that nonetheless speak to the man on the street. Bilbao has become a pilgrimage point for those who, until now, had little interest in architecture. Working class Basque couples arrive toting children on weekends. The cultural elite veer off their regular flight paths so they can tell friends that they, too, have seen the building in the flesh. Gehry has become, in the eyes of a world attuned to celebrity, the great America architect, and, in the process, he has brought hope to an entire profession. (1998)

Tracing the story of the creation of the Bilbao Museum reveals the unfolding nature of the design process, with its emphasis on experimentation and iteration and its comfort with ambiguity. Gehry's first sketches are on pieces of hotel stationery. They are "fast scrawls and mere annotations…the hand functions as an immediate tool of the mind," Gehry said. Later, on an airplane, as the design evolves, the sketches begin to capture the basics of his scheme for the site. Gehry explains:

> I start drawing sometimes, not knowing where it is going….It's like feeling your way along in the dark, anticipating that something will come out usually. I become a voyeur of my own thoughts as they develop, and wander

---

15. See Muschamp (1998); Ouroussoff (1998), p. 18; and C. Van Bruggen, Frank O. Gehry: Guggenheim Museum Bilbao. (New York Guggenheim Museum Publications, 1997: 33, 31, 71, 103, 135, 104, 130.

about them. Sometimes I say boy, here it is, it's coming. I understand it. I get all excited and from there I'll move to the models, and the models drain all of the energy, and need information on scale and relationships that you can't conceive in totality in drawings. The drawings are ephemeral. The models are the specific; they then become like the sketches in the next phase. (Van Bruggen, 1997)

The models change scale and materials as the project progresses, becoming increasingly detailed, and moving from paper to plastic to wood to industrial foam. Throughout, the process remains iterative. In the end, the process from first sketch into final building remains one of unfolding:

In the first sketch, I put a bunch of principles down. Then I become self-critical of those images and those principles, and they evoke the next set of responses. And as each piece unfolds, I make the models bigger and bigger, bringing into focus more elements and more pieces of the puzzle. And once I have the beginning, a toehold into where I'm going, then I want to examine the parts in more detail. And those evolve, and at some point I stop, because that's it. I don't come to a conclusion, but I think there's a certain reality of pressure to get the thing done that I accept. (Van Bruggen, 1997)

One of the keys to successful design that we see at work in Gehry's story is the intersection of possibilities and constraints. Both of these elements are key in the design process—and sequence matters. Gehry starts with the possibilities question—he lets himself dream. He then tests his dreams, and uses the feedback from the tests to reformulate the dreams. In the way the design evolves—in the familiar kind of "two steps forward, one step back" kind of way. He is patient with the indeterminacy and inefficiency of the unfolding process—and persistent in continuing the iterative cycles of dreaming and testing until he finds the dream that works. Pushing too hard on the

Leaders' desire for control and certainty can be the biggest obstacle to creating the kinds of conversations that produce compelling visions of the future.

constraints too early drives out the dreams and destroys the truly innovative possibilities; ignoring the constraints for too long takes us down blind alleys and produces designs that don't work in real life. Successfully using the tension between the two to drive the design forward is perhaps the most critical design skill of all.

Business leaders have much to learn, I believe, from Gehry's description of the iterative and unpredictable design process. Leaders' desire for control and certainty can be the biggest obstacle to creating the kinds of conversations that produce compelling visions of the future.

And I use the word *conversation* quite deliberately. For far too long we have held onto the belief that vision and strategy creation were only the job of the leader, the last bastions of executive prerogative, formulated on senior management retreats and then carried down the mountain, like the 10 commandments, to be delivered to the faithful waiting anxiously below. But compelling visions are not the result of pronouncements, but of persuasion. Commitment emerges from dialogues, not directives. The successful leader in a time of change is always a *storyteller* who engages the listener along the way and invites them into the story as it unfolds.

Conjuring is a vastly under-appreciated leadership skill. Too often the search for vision is pursued as though there was a single, unique "holy grail" to be found, with the belief that, once discovered, the "rightness" of the solution will be as obvious to everyone else as it is to the leader. But because designs are always inventions, leaders can never prove the "rightness" of any single vision to others. Instead, they must *persuade* others that a given vision is worth pursuing, helping others to see the possibilities and constraints along the way.

One of the most powerful examples of this that I have seen was provided by one of the regional vice-presidents of one of the largest insurance firms in the United States. Concerned about the internal focus that seemed to dominate his managers' attention in the wake of reorganization, along with the confusion that multiple simultaneous change initiatives had created, he devised a novel exercise in strategic thinking to open their annual forecasting and review session. He began by writing on an overhead the familiar financial formula that defined performance in their business:

Premiums – Losses – Administrative Costs = Operating Surplus/(Deficit)

Next, he listed five different equations, all in the above formula. All unlabeled, four of these represented the firm's major competitors. Another represented the performance of the firm itself, all for the preceding year. He asked his managers to identify which firm each equation described, and why. This challenge set the stage for a lively, engaging 30 minutes of dialogue among the managers present, a conversation rich with shared insights, disagreements, and differing assumptions. It was not a test—the vice-president facilitated the discussion, asked probing questions, and acted as scribe. When each of the equations had been labeled accurately, he turned to the firm's own and asked his managers to consider how and where each of the change initiatives underway would impact their equation and, in turn, their strategic positioning vis-à-vis competition.

That 60-minute session remains, in my mind, one of the most strategic conversations that I have seen an executive lead. Managers left the room with a more coherent sense of the strategic imperatives facing the firm, the way the current initiatives underway contributed to meeting those imperatives, and why their role in moving these forward was essential. They experienced, as a result of that conversation, a deepened sense of both understanding and urgency. They saw the "big picture," understood their role in it more clearly, and were better able to look for opportunities to both move the changes along, and to help their people see why they were important. There were no outside facilitators involved, no fancy new techniques, no posh retreat or executive education setting. They met in the cafeteria, and they talked openly with each other about an important set of issues. They were asked to think, and to listen to each other as well as their boss. They were invited to participate, rather than to take notes, or to wait for the Q&A. They left the room better strategic thinkers, better able to participate in the design of their organization's future.

This role of "lead conjurer" is not an easy one—especially when leading the possibilities conversation. Frank Gehry tells another instructive story about the difficulty of leading others to think about the future in creative ways. At one point, he explains, he was engaged in designing a new faculty building for MIT and a home for schizophrenic teenagers, simultaneously. As is always his practice, he began both design processes by having a conversation with each group, asking them what they envisioned their ideal future space would look like. One of the teenagers was particularly captivating in her detailed description of the hoped-for space. "It wasn't until she described the crack in the ceiling over my head," Gehry recalls, "that I realized that she had just spent 10 minutes describing the space as it existed today." What was even more disheartening, Gehry explained, was realizing that the MIT faculty had done exactly the same thing in his conversations with them—"only it was a lot harder to detect," he argues, "because they weren't mentally ill."

Designing Leader Skills

Few development efforts help leaders understand and lead a design process, which requires making the difficult transition from being strategic thinkers themselves to leading strategic conversations in their organizations, a skill which our insurance executive above demonstrated so well.

Becoming a good designer of visions and strategies requires developing a specific set of skills:

- the ability to clarify and articulate both the purpose and the values at work, which are the foundation of any design;
- the ability to engage others in the design conversation, and to be patient and persistent as it evolves, taking various twists and turns;
- the ability to listen, to take on the perspectives of others, to tolerate the ambiguity and chaos characteristic of all creative processes, and to trust the process of conversation itself
- a capacity for conjuring—for describing the future, unfolding it in a way that makes it vivid and compelling.

As educators, none of these attributes is wholly new to us. Most leadership development efforts recognize the importance of listening, of perspective taking, of values clarification. Some are even beginning to pay attention to the importance of storytelling.

What the design metaphor highlights is the way in which these individual leadership skills need to come together in a participative process that often puts the leader in a new role—that of facilitator and boundary-setter of a design conversation. This is the contribution that design offers: identifying and developing the leadership mindset and skill set needed to guide organizations through the value-driven, often messy and chaotic process by which it conjures its own future—resulting in powerful strategic visions and leadership that matters.

That great design matters is clear—consider the differing reactions elicited by the Golden Gate and the Oakland Bay bridges. Both offer reliable transport across the water separating San Francisco and its neighbors. The similarity ends there. The Golden Gate enthralls. It sweeps, it symbolizes, it inspires music, art, and myth. The Oakland Bay Bridge works. If we aspire to building visions that feel to employees more like the Golden Gate than the Oakland Bay, we need leaders that design.

Jeanne M. Liedtka

Jeanne M. Liedtka is executive director of the Darden School's Batten Institute, a research center focused on developing thought leadership in the areas of entrepreneurship and corporate innovation. Jeanne is also a faculty member at the University of Virginia's Darden Graduate School of Business, and former chief learning officer at United Technologies Corporation where she was responsible for overseeing all activities associated with corporate learning and development for the *Fortune* 50 corporation, including executive education, career development processes, employer-sponsored education, and learning portal and web-based activities. It was during her time with United Technologies that Jeanne began interacting with InterClass. At Darden, where she formerly served as associate dean of the MBA program, Jeanne works with both MBAs and executives in the areas of strategic thinking, collaboration, and leading growth. Her passion is around exploring how organizations can engage employees at every level in thinking creatively about the design of powerful futures.

Jeanne received her DBA in Management Policy from Boston University and her MBA from the Harvard Business School. She has been involved in the corporate strategy field since beginning her career as a strategy consultant for the Boston Consulting Group.

NETWORK LEADERSHIP

By Eric E. Vogt

President, InterClass

Business keeps increasing in complexity. We used to be able to simply visit with our customer, have a conversation, make the sale, and ship the product. Now, we play phone tag with voicemail, create long email chains, have several conference calls with the potential customer, then struggle to find a time for a conference call with our OWN extended enterprise to articulate a solution in collaboration with people who seldom are in our own span of control or time zone, which subsequently will be shopped by the customer against competition on the Internet, and analyzed electronically for any weakness by a host of

> *A network leader is someone who understands how to construct, inspire, and nurture networks of people and networks of organizations toward a mutual purpose, independent of formal lines of authority.*

people we have never met. And all this happens in a compressed Internet timeframe, while the volatility of the stock market and the ambiguity of international events change the landscape daily. And we wonder why corporate burnout is on the rise.

Complexity is here to stay. What can change is our leadership philosophy and behaviors. Successful leaders in this century will be effective

network leaders. I believe that effective network leaders will populate the most successful organizations in this century.

The evidence from InterClass suggests that indeed, the capabilities of network leaders have been desperately needed in recent years. Consider the following challenges we have encountered:

- A new partner of a global business, insurance, and financial consulting company has to develop a new strategy and develop consensus on a global basis in a firm with 3,000 partners, including many new partners from a recent acquisition, which had a very different culture.

- An engineering manager of a multinational in vertical transportation has to develop an innovative technical response to a new competitor's offering in a highly compressed timeframe with a team that reports to seven different executives.

- A senior marketing executive at a global pharmaceutical company has to develop a coherent, coordinated and rapid response to a competitor's challenge to their top-selling drug, working with professionals from seventeen different European countries, all of whom also have competing priorities.

These challenges, and others which I am sure the reader can articulate, underscore the need for capable network leaders now. In my experience, all of the interesting, challenging work today happens across boundaries—geographical, organizational, disciplinary, and cultural boundaries—in an environment where traditional command and control behaviors are meaningless. The challenge we have lies in the selection and development of network leaders, capable of thriving in this complex environment. This chapter will examine this challenge in greater detail. What is a Network Leader? What are the competencies of a Network Leader? How do we develop effective network leaders?

NETWORK LEADERSHIP: A STORY

The Massachusetts Software Council (now the Mass Technology Leadership Council) is a powerful force in the New England software industry, and a frequent voice in Washington. Over five hundred and fifty software companies are active members of the council, attending meetings regularly to understand new technologies, converse with colleagues, identify trends and source the raw material of the industry: fresh ideas. The leadership of the Council has met Massachusetts' senators, as well as Congressmen, the governor, and Alan Greenspan, with the intent of shaping the political landscape to support the growth of the software industry. Each year the trustees of the Council meet in a day-long off-site to explore the most critical emerging trends in the software and related industries—from wireless networks and the venture capital overhang, to nanotechnology and genomics. The Council operates as a vibrant, pulsating knowledge network, connecting the people and the ideas, which will generate the future of the industry.

Was it always this way? No, not at all. Before 1985, the concept of the Council did not even exist, much less the network or the activity. Do networks just happen? Or are they led? Do they just emerge when the time is ripe? Or must a leader issue the call? But how can you lead a network without authority?

In the case of the Council, I had the privilege to observe the leadership conversations that led to the articulation and formation of the software council. Like most innovations, it started in a "what if" conversation. Jacquie Morby, leading Venture Capitalist and legendary networker, had told me about a young, articulate software CEO that she thought I would like to meet. Richard Rabins had started Alpha Software three years before, about the time I had founded MicroMentor in 1983. We agreed to meet for breakfast at the Meridien, in downtown Boston. A lively conversation ensued over eggs Benedict.

Towards the end of our breakfast, after we had empathetically listened to each other's business concerns, the conversation moved to, **"What's next?"** and to "What might we contribute to the world on a larger scale than simply one business?" In that wonderful dance of a co-creative conversation we wondered what would happen if Massachusetts were to market software in the way Florida markets orange juice. Sure, the climate of Florida ostensibly makes it ideal for growing oranges. But the intellectual climate of Massachusetts makes it ideal for growing software companies. At first a playful idea, we then moved to **"What if?"** "What if we were to create a community of software CEO's?" "What if we could convince the leadership of the commonwealth to play an active role in marketing Massachusetts software?" In that playful conversation, the concept of The "Massachusetts Software Union" was born. We subsequently drafted the two-page white paper.

Observation:
Network leadership requires fluency in co-creative conversations.

By definition, a co-creative conversation only happens with trust, listening, and a willingness to build on each other's ideas, without proprietary ownership of the result.

The next step was to approach the leadership of the commonwealth. Naïve myself in the ways of politics, I invited Josh Posner, a friend and savvy consumer activist from Mass Fair Share to join the conversation. The three of us met with the then Lt. Governor Evelyn Murphy, who carried the torch of economic development. Evelyn had frequently been quoted as saying that "Massachusetts has only two abundant natural resources: universities and rocks." Clearly, software was one of the growth industries in the commonwealth, which emanated from the former. The gentle coaching from Evelyn was clear, "Great idea, I am happy to introduce you to Governor Dukakis, but you need a few more software CEO's before you can really begin to speak for the industry." It was time to go recruiting.

I immediately thought of Mitch Kapor of Lotus, and John Cullinane, the man who invented packaged software, but who else? In 1984, the now ubiquitous Mass Technology Leadership Council Directory did not exist. Indeed, it would not even be conceived of until 1987. So I networked, I called Esther.

Esther Dyson had recently taken over Ben Rosen's newsletter of the electronics industry and had the prescient vision to re-position it as a newsletter serving the infant PC industry. "Well," said Esther, the folks who might respond to this sort of idea are Dan Bricklin of Software Arts, David Solomont of BPS, Mort Rosenthal of Corporate Software, and Mike Kinkead of Saddlebrook." I invited them all to have dinner with Richard Rabins and me to explore the notion of a "Massachusetts Software Union."

> ### *Observation:*
> ### Network leadership thrives on evangelism.

I thought the evening would elicit more gracious, reflective "What if," conversations like our first breakfast. Instead, it was tumultuous. I discovered we had eight software CEOs in the room, and at least twelve opinions. What would we do? How would we finance it? Who are the members? How large should it be? Would we engage in political lobbying activities? Of course, I had a very clear vision: only software CEOs, each paying dues of $1,000 per year, thirty to forty members, no political lobbying, and closed meetings to help each other think through business problems. My idea was that it should be sort of a blend between the YPO and group therapy. Nobody agreed with me. And, nobody agreed with each other. But somehow, we did decide to have another dinner meeting. The attractive forces of the potential union won out over the centrifugal forces of young egos.

> ### *Observation:*
> ### Network leadership requires a compelling common purpose.

We had several more dinner meetings, hosted by various members of the fledgling union. We found enough common ground to lose the "union" label which had "labor union" overtones for some, and find a more appropriate name, the Massachusetts Software Council. [In 2005 the Massachusetts Software Council merged with the New England Business and Technology Association to form the Mass Technology Leadership Council]. The momentum was enough to call Evelyn Murphy back and ask for a meeting with Governor Dukakis. The following month we found ourselves in the Governor's office as Mike Dukakis listened and encouraged our formative activities. Mike had also invited John Cullinane and Mitch Kapor to the meeting, knowing that the added muscle would help the effort. The governor's quiet agenda, I learned later, was to replace the conservative voice of the Mass High Tech Council with a fresh, more liberal voice of the emerging Software Council. The High Tech Council was predominantly hardware CEO's in their fifties, who were fighting many of Dukakis' democratic initiatives. In contrast, we were predominantly in our thirties, and already liberal and more democratic in terms of political leaning. On one level, that was fine with us, it provided added momentum. However, I worried about my proposed apolitical agenda for the young network organization.

Observation:
Network leadership is developed through mentors.

After another three rounds of tumultuous dinners and dialogue, a structure began to emerge from the chaotic conversation. John Cullinane's steady hand and experienced advice shaped our early principles: Our primary purpose: Information and Networking. Annual dues: $250 per company, plus $5 per employee. Aim for building membership as high as possible. Focus upon industry issues, but do not shy away from politics. And, add the word "Computer" to the name of the organization to clearly differentiate us from the garment industry's use of the word "software!" For his wisdom, we elected John chairman. Most of the early policies we adopted were 180 degrees away from my original point of view, and I was flexible and energetic, just learning to be a network leader. So, I was elected president, and the real journey began.

Observation:
**As with lab scientists, network leadership happens
in the doing. And, in reality, network leaders are anointed
rather than appointed.**

Twelve months after the original breakfast conversation with Richard Rabins, the inaugural breakfast meeting of the Council was held. Mitch Kapor and Governor Dukakis provided the keynotes, and 85 software CEO's came out of the woodwork, when we had only expected 30! The network was formally born, and we enthusiastically aspired to have 200 members someday. None of us imagined what the Council would become in twenty-two years, with more than 550 corporate members and a voice in Washington.

> *Observation:*
> **Network leaders are more like a stream bed[16] than a railroad;**
> **they channel the energy, yet adapt and change with time.**

HOW IS NETWORK LEADERSHIP DIFFERENT?

Simply stated, the easy problems have all been solved. Our world today is more complex, inter-connected, and fast-paced than it was twenty years ago by an order of magnitude. The kind of leader we need to deal with the challenge of this next century is a network leader. By network leader, I mean a leader who is capable of

- constructing effective networks
- inspiring networks into action
- nurturing networks.

At first you may say to yourself, "Sure, sure, this is like leading with influence, we did that in the 1990s," but influence is very different from networking. Influence skills are useful; indeed, they are necessary, but far from sufficient. Influence skills are typically designed to allow leaders to cajole action out of colleagues in the same organization, where the basic mission and values are shared. Influence skills are also articulated from the perspective that "I have the answer, and I need to get the others to think it was their idea."

Network leaders have to build a very different kind of capability. Network leaders will more frequently be working between large organizations or among smaller ones. Network leaders will be fluent in the art of blending perspectives and engaging in co-creative conversations that lead to a very different perspective than the one they may have held on the way into the conversation. Network leaders are part scientist, part evangelist, part therapist.

---

16. A **stream bed** is the channel bottom of a stream or river or creek; the physical confine of the normal water flow. The nature of any stream bed is always a function of the flow dynamics and the local geologic materials influenced by that flow.

What are Network Leadership Competencies?

Part of the answer to this question might be derived empirically. From the brief history above about the creation of the Massachusetts Software Council, we can make the following observations:

- Network leadership requires fluency in co-creative conversations.
- Network leadership thrives on evangelism.
- Network leadership requires a compelling common purpose.
- Network leadership is developed through mentors.
- Network leadership happens in the doing.
- Network leaders are anointed rather than appointed.
- Network leaders are more like a streambed than a railroad; they channel the energy, yet adapt and change with time.

Beyond these observations, how else might we explore the competencies of network leadership? What are some current examples? Let's take Linus Torvalds, creator of the Linux operating system, acknowledged leader of the open source community, and architect of a social and intellectual phenomenon without equal in today's interconnected world. What are the characteristics of this network leader? Most observers, including Linus himself if he were not so self-effacing, would probably list the following characteristics of this unique network leader:

- Clarity of purpose
- Integrity
- Trust
- Open communication
- Unwavering principles
- Passion
- Listening
- Serving others
- A focus on giving, rather than getting
- Filtering knowledge through others

In his autobiography, *Just for Fun: The Story of an Accidental Revolutionary*, Torvalds describes how he simply set out to build a better operating system because the one he was using was so clumsy. His passion was for the challenge of creating higher performance at the operating system so that the machine could support more interesting applications, like multi-tasking, simultaneous disk calls, and, ironically, effective networking. His aim was NOT making money, yet he was supportive of others making money supporting his invention. His mode of operating was to trust the network, and to behave in a way that ensured the network would trust him. All of Torvalds' work is issued under the General Public License, or GPL, which dictates that anyone may have the source code, as long as all improvements are contributed back for everyone to review. This is the concept of "copy left" rather than the traditional "copyright."

Linux improved quickly, based upon the feedback from the growing network. The fact that this was a communal effort, unencumbered by ownership issues and financial greed, supported the rapid growth of the network. As first hundreds, and then thousands of programmers worldwide, began to work on solving specific problems and improving Linux. Torvalds delegated the filtering process to proven, trusted hacker colleagues, but retained the final decision of which code went into the next version of the Linux kernel himself. This process is clear, communicated, and respected by what is now a large global community. Furthermore, the final decision is always simply based upon performance of the code, not on playing favorites or responding to political pressure. The Linux community is a global hacker meritocracy. And the currency of the realm is the ultimate: **community reputation.**

How Do We Select And Develop network leaders?

I begin with the question of selection. I have come to believe that, indeed, you cannot always make a silk purse from a sow's ear. Network leaders require a starting capacity to hold ambiguity, to listen and integrate, and to inspire without ego. These are not always common traits. I am reminded of the work of Eliot Jaques (Requisite Organization), who spent forty years helping large organizations locate and develop talent. Eliot started with an assessment process to determine the capacity of the candidate to hold cognitive complexity. This is a distinction he derived by looking at some of the world's great leaders, particularly those who were able to see and make changes happen well beyond their own lifetime. On a simplistic level, you might assess a candidate's ability to hold cognitive complexity through a diagnostic question like, "What is your opinion of euthanasia?" One answer might be, "Well, it is illegal." Another answer might be, "Well, euthanasia is a complicated conversation, which in the end must strive to balance ethics, law, society, and human rights." I will leave it to you to judge which candidate might have a higher level of cognitive complexity. Perhaps you can identify these two different leaders in your own organization.

Eliot Jaques had only a few large organizations as clients. One was the U.S. Army where he identified a young major with a high ability to hold cognitive complexity. Eliot then went out of his way to make sure that the Army gave this young major the career opportunities to stretch himself, work with mentors, and build his network. Eliot's strategy worked pretty well. I would have to say that General Colin Powell developed pretty well as a network leader. Secretary of State Colin Powell may have run into a network leadership road block also described by Eliot Jacques: namely, having a longer time horizon and a greater understanding of complexity then the people he was working for—in other words—he could see what was comin'. I suspect there is yet more to emerge from the actions of citizen Colin Powell.

So, I do conclude that selection is key. And I would challenge you in your organization to begin to look at how you might select your network leader candidates. Look for those who catalyze a conversation, which moves across the organizational boundaries. Look for those who both call out and serve a high purpose. Look for those with the capacity to tell a story about future possibility that travels. Look for those who listen at least as much as they talk. Look for those who can weave multiple strands of ambiguity into a coherent framework for a constructive conversation.

Once you have selected a group of potential network leaders, the next value add is to construct their development experience. A big hairy project that moves across the boundaries of the organization, and requires the skills of the scientist, evangelist, and therapist is certainly a great way to start. This is particularly true since a network leader not only needs these skills to operate effectively, but also needs the opportunities to build his or her network of relationships in the organization. I would also add to the development plan of your identified network leaders the experience of leading an industry association or community organization. There is nothing so humbling as trying to make something happen without having the authority. In this context, it is interesting to speculate about the degree to which we might add the model of effective political leaders to our competencies for the optimal network leader. What are the skills and competencies of Tony Blair that we might want to capture and develop in our own leaders as well?

As with Colin Powell, it is also critical to locate the network mentors you have in your organization and line them up with your candidates. Who are your mentors for these network leaders? Do you need to look outside of the organization? Many people are bemoaning the fact that we are losing so much of our experienced executive talent these days to layoffs and early retirement. Who are the mentors who have "left" the organization who might be intrigued with the opportunity to coach an emerging network leader through the quagmire of the organization?

A New Mindset and New Behaviors

Developing effective network leaders requires both a mindset change and a behavioral change. The difference from the leadership role of the president of the United States, to the leadership role of the secretary of state, is an apt metaphor for the change in mindset required. As a network leader, everything happens through listening, engaging, and enrolling others in the possibility of a better tomorrow. Direct commands are few, and the currency of the network is built through the **Three Rs of network leadership:**

Respect   **Reciprocity**   **Reputation**

The recipe for behavioral change is much more easily said than done: Give to the network, it will respond unpredictably and abundantly in kind. Keep your focus on the purpose. Build relationships across the boundaries. Disengage your ego. Tell stories that travel well. Keep your promises and build trust.

And of the truly great leader the people will say, "We did it ourselves."

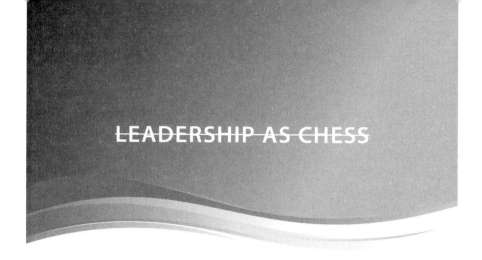

LEADERSHIP AS CHESS

By Mike Wenger

Consultant, Wenger & Wenger Consulting

Introduction

In my experience, it is always misleading to attempt to illuminate leadership by shining attention on the leader while shunting to the background the people led and the context in which the alleged leadership took place. Certainly, the collective changes the leader as much as the leader changes the collective. To really understand leadership, you have to articulate a dynamic, holistic, and long-term view of a leader as an individual responding within a constant stream of other people's actions and of unfolding changes. Each day, the leader is greeted by a new arena different from the day before. Some days the differences are subtle; others days the differences are glaring. In the complex environment of the modern corporation, other leaders are working on their own projects, more or less under the overall coherence of corporate strategies. The arena for everyone changes as plans (and non-plans) unfold. To understand leadership, we need to step back from the "leader" and view "leader in the leadership project."

For the past 30 years, as I have practiced, researched, studied, and taught leadership, I have looked for ways to think about the topic in this dynamic and holistic way. I have looked to architecture, music, gardening, biology, cybernetics, sports, games, and religion for suitable metaphors and illustrative examples. Of all of these, I have found what I read of chess to be a particularly useful balance between science and art, discipline and creativity, predictability and randomness, intention and surprise. This metaphor captures a lot of my experienced reality of leadership. Chess is a way to think about leadership without overstating the power of one leader or ignoring the fact that one person can make a powerful difference.

In this chapter, I will use the metaphor and a four-year project[17] in which I am a leader to examine ways to think about leading in a business transformation. I want to emphasize action and reaction between a leader and the collective and to recognize the critical shifts in context that occur over time because of those interactions. The idea of a chess game—with an opening, a middle game, and an end game—gives me insight into my actions, my feelings, the changes that go on around me, and my changing leadership role. This metaphor has helped me plan my actions and anticipate outcomes. It has helped me understand more clearly some of the unanticipated situations that emerged. It provided useful conceptual models to critical phase changes throughout a three-year leadership project.[18]

This is the story about a very common business leadership challenge: how to take an organization and quickly move it to an industry-leading position in a new and emerging business arena. Changing a business from what **has** been successful in the past to new modes that **will be** successful in the future is a basic business leadership task, faced everyday by thousands of executives. In my case, the project was to help transform a very successful business unit, the training business of a successful global IT company. The Educational Services unit had grown rapidly over the previous seven years, partly due to the burgeoning IT industry and the exceptional growth of the corporation, but also because of an explicit and aggressive expansion of the unit's portfolio.

Background: The Transformation Challenge

The Educational Services vice president and his executive team had, over recent years, added a variety of learning planning, skills

---

17. The time period of this project is roughly 2000–2004.
18. I am not a player of chess, only a reader about chess.

assessment, and certification services, and begun to develop a technology-based delivery and service capability. Nearly all sales were still focused on a fairly limited subset of IT training. After nearly seven years of deliberate growth along this line, the limiting factor for further growth became the scalability of the business. Simply, with our existing model of business and technology, we could not profitably grow the traditional education consulting services and bricks and mortar training much beyond the size and scope we had attained. Further, our most important customers—those organizations who engage in large, long-term contracts for employee skills development—were increasingly turning to suppliers who could package broad subject coverage, integrative education services, and technology for training and training management. If we maintained a targeted, niche-subject-matter focus and had no substantial technology offer, our relationship with these customers would increasingly be mediated by emerging third-party "solutions" providers. The solutions providers would control the strategic relationship with our customers. Clearly, this would ultimately drive us to commodity status and to sacrifice margins. For a profit center like us, that is a bad situation. Even more critically, it would also cede influence over emerging learning technology and infrastructure design just at the start of the coming decades of industry transformation. For a corporation founded on technology leadership, this was simply untenable. To respond to this strategic situation, we decided to stake out a strong position in the broader training and skills management industry and become a leader in IT infrastructure for that industry.

Achieving our goal would entail building a portfolio of extended solutions with multiple services, multiple delivery modes, and a strong technology foundation. My charter was to build from our base and lead the strategic initiative to become a significant force in the emerging eLearning industry.[19] This would entail rapidly embracing new technologies and processes; quickly developing a new market position in the customer, analyst, and press communities; and changing the attitude of the existing

---

19. At the time, we (like everyone in the industry) used the term "eLearning." I now use the less glamorous, but more accurate term, "Technology-Enhanced Learning," to reflect that learning design today blends the use of electronic networks, multiple computing, and communications devices, and traditional physical world learning modes. For consistency, I use "eLearning" throughout this chapter.

workforce, who were born and bred in the world of instructor-led classroom training.

Though this challenge seemed special to us, it is a very common story. Like countless businesses before us, we were trying to bring fundamental change to our organization. Ultimately, this would require hiring new people, establishing new groups with new charters, negotiating new roles, creating new products and services, developing new business processes, and building an aggressive marketing campaign to gain mind share with customers and industry analysts. This kind of story is going on in hundreds of businesses around the world and in every industry imaginable. A common leadership challenge, we might call it the "transforming a business" leadership challenge. During the past three years, I was a leader, along with many others,[20] of an effort to meet this challenge.

The Opening

In this position there are a half-dozen starting moves for White that are considered good. In reply to each of these, Black has three or four good replies when again White usually has a number of possibilities—and so on. These are the Openings—the play of both sides at the beginning of a game in which the players are repeating (whether they know it or not) the moves that have been played many times before.[21]

The moves for this sort of business transformation are very well known and taught in business schools throughout the world.[22] It entails understanding the industry, assessing risks and opportunities, deciding the strategy, setting a vision, and building a team with focus, capability,

---

20. In a first person account, this critical point may become obscured, so I will emphasize it here. Without the combined effort and contribution of the other executives in the business unit and throughout the corporation, I could not have had any success. Further, as in all important transformations, the countless leaders in individual contributor roles are key. I was, like all "leaders," one of many.

21. David B. Pritchard. *Begin Chess*, 2nd ed. (New York: Penguin, 1991), p. 105.

22. From my experience as an MBA student, a business executive trying to apply what I learned for my MBA, and a faculty member teaching MBAs, one of my concerns with business schools is that they tend to teach **only** the openings. As you will see below, I believe the later stages of the transformation game are harder and, in many ways, more important to ultimate success.

and resources. As we pursued our opening, we faced the common decision. Should we grow internally or through acquisition? Ultimately we chose acquisition. Our opening took almost exactly one year.

There is nearly a cookbook quality to the opening in chess. Each side follows predictable and commonly known sequential steps for the initial moves. But this does not mean that the opening (in chess or in business) is mindless or that anyone can do it equally well. Rather, the point is that the opening game is well-trod territory. We understand the general approaches and techniques, and know which tools to apply to our specific situation. To illustrate the point, I will focus on four traditional opening moves for business transformation: simple focused vision, building the team, messaging the industry shapers, and growth through acquisition.

Simple, focused vision. Boiling the complexity of a major transformation down to a simple, easy-to-repeat, compelling statement is a well-known leadership technique. In our case, the opening challenge was clear. I did not know the details of **how** we would become an eLearning industry leader, but little in-depth analysis was required to know the general pattern of **what** we must do. Beyond a limited image as a provider of product-specific training, our corporation was not known in the learning industry. Neither were we known as a player in eLearning technology and design. Further, the emerging industry was a "wild west," with many poorly run companies and eager, but confused, customers. A significant consolidation was inevitable in the eLearning industry and we had an opportunity to take an important position in that consolidation.

Given our starting position, we had a straightforward set of things to do in order to become an important industry leader. I articulated our game strategy in a presentation I gave soon after I was hired. I said we had a simple three-point strategy: 1) get in the game fast, 2) stay in the game during the industry shakeout, and 3) become an industry leader. I repeated some version of this simple 3-step mantra hundreds of times over the subsequent months. In my mind, this also mapped nicely onto the opening, middle, and end game of chess. I anticipated the transformation would be a three-to-four year process.

Building the team. When we began the game, no set of employees was specifically dedicated to the new business. We had employees devoted to existing operations, including classroom, custom solutions, and consulting, and a nascent technology-based product area, which included several small groups and individuals working on web-based products and services. Almost immediately, we began to build the team. We gathered everyone who was working on web products and services into "the eLearning team" and hired new people with additional skills and capabilities. Setting up and building the team took nearly a year.

I knew and stated explicitly that this team was provisional in the sense that at some point in the future when the overall organization was transformed, eLearning would not, could not, and should not be a separate part of the organization. Our activities would become mainstream, and, consequently, we would have to merge back into the mainstream as well. Consequently, we created job descriptions that were good enough to justify new hires and focus our effort, but we recognized the jobs would not endure. In fact, I told everyone that we would have to revisit our job descriptions and roles at least every six months. Naturally, change agent skills and the ability to deal with ambiguity were important aspects of everyone's job when they joined the eLearning team.

Messaging the industry shapers. As in most corporations, we had strong corporate public relations and analyst relations teams. They are skilled professionals with industry contacts, established processes, and effective planning skills to connect our corporate activities to industry shapers. If the business unit can supply the vision, focus, and spokespeople, then public relations and analyst relations will help craft and deliver the message. Success in this area required I develop a strong coalition of marketing, consulting, and other senior executives, to help develop our message and to take it to the world. By the end of the year, we had tested our messages, engaged important industry shapers, widely announced our intentions, and established a network of forums and associations. The analysts were receptive and even eager in some cases. They were also skeptical enough to take a wait-and-see stance.

Growth through Acquisition. We faced a classic "build or buy" decision. As in all such decisions, the trade-offs were well known. An acquisition—a buy decision—offered the advantages of rapidly gaining technology and talent, unequivocal control of the technology, market presence, and a customer pipeline. It also required the cost of the deal, the effort and cost to integrate the organization post-deal, and the continued impact of the goodwill write-down. For a business unit of a larger corporation, of course, there is the added challenge of the pressure for payback on the investment. With the build option, growth comes in a much more controlled way, but faces the known disadvantages of finding and recruiting talent, building and testing the products and processes, and gradually building market presence. An additional factor in our thinking reflected the turbulent nature of the industry. If we relied on partners for the underlying technology, we faced concerns over control of that technology in the volatile, soon-to-consolidate market. In the end, as we worked though all these issues and trade-offs, we found an attractive acquisition target, gained corporate board approval, and successfully pursued an acquisition.

Throughout the opening, my leadership role and tasks were clear to me. I worked with the executive team to craft a clear and focused vision. I established, focused, and motivated the eLearning team. I was the main spokesperson and business lead for the acquisition analysis, deal, and integration teams.

The end of our opening was quite clearly marked when, after just over twelve months, we closed on the acquisition of a strong, well-regarded startup. We had a massive expansion of talent, technology, and customer potential. And we made a splash in the industry—the industry shapers knew and reported that we were "in the game." We were just ahead of the coming industry consolidation.

The Middle Game

The middle game is the battle proper in which you have to find your own way helped by a few guiding principles and your own experience. . . If you start the game well, you will enter the middle game with confidence and if you understand the end game you will be confident of where you are going in the middle game.[23]

For me as a leader, perhaps the most enlightening insight of the chess metaphor is the stark difference between the opening and the middle game. This is where the relative clarity of well-known moves, coupled with the intrinsic excitement of starting the game, gives way quite abruptly to

---

23. Pritchard, p. 126

a new phase. After all the work, all the team building, all the airline miles, and all the success, you have not yet won. In fact, you are nowhere near winning. All you have done is "set up the board," and hopefully put yourself in a position of advantage for the coming phase.

The overall vision remained the same. Our goal for the middle game was to "stay in the game during the industry shakeout." Simply, we needed to create a strong, sustainable business as quickly as possible from the parts we had collected. To do this, we needed to maintain, retain, and expand mindshare and commitment from customers, industry shapers, and the executives of both the business unit and the corporation. We had to create new business processes, new products, and new services in the new combined organization. This drive to create a sustainable business was the most basic guiding principle for me, which I again tried to articulate in a simple, focused vision. I preached four themes for the coming year: 1) product improvement, 2) process development, 3) partnership growth, and 4) customer engagement. For me, ensuring that we accomplished these four points would be the focus for the middle game.

I felt confident as we entered the middle game. Of course, I did not know the details necessary to achieve the goals, but the four themes seemed to offer the same clarity that we had in the opening moves. I knew it was a new phase and I knew that my role as leader would be different. However, I underestimated how different the middle game would be. In the middle game, there is intrinsically much more variability and unpredictability. This is where each game is most unique.

One clear example of this difference is the role of market competitors. In the opening, market competitors are important as factors to analyze. You identify a competitive strategic position and pursue it. In our get-in-the-game opening, we did not need to win customers. We were simply moving into position. But in the middle game, we had to actually engage the competition, win customers, and establish market position as quickly as possible. The competitors suddenly took on a new role and offered a new set of challenges. In the middle game, the opportunities become very specific—focusing on specific customers with specific needs and very specific offers from the competition. Success in the middle game demanded strong execution of sales and delivery much more than the simple strategic analysis required in the opening.

The middle game offers a triple challenge because you have to go to market with a business that is not yet fully transformed. Simultaneously, you must lead 1) in the long-term context of the original transformation, and 2) in the intermediate term context of building new processes, tools, products, and capabilities; and 3) in the short-term context of going to market with what you have. When opening a business transformation, you are setting the stage and collecting the parts. In the middle game, you have to execute against the expectations of the new business as you build it, solidifying a sound foothold both in the market and within the corporation. I found the middle game to be a much greater challenge than the opening. I believe we all did.

There were several aspects of the middle game that I anticipated. One was the fact that moving from the opening to the middle game would be an emotional letdown. The letdown comes from the nature of the work required in the middle game. There is rarely as much glory in building disciplined, reliable product program management as there is in developing a cool new vision and technology. Nor is there as much visibility given to the hard work and contribution of integrating the people, cultures, processes, and products after an acquisition as there is to making the deal in the first place. This is a shame, because ultimate success demands winning the middle game and these business fundamentals are characteristic middle game activities. While the opening is loud, visible, and exciting, the middle game is quiet, invisible, and simply hard work.

While the opening is loud, visible, and exciting, the middle game is quiet, invisible, and simply hard work.

In business, much of the glory goes to the leaders who are good at the opening game. However, in many ways the real heroes are the leaders who excel at the middle game. I anticipated that my biggest contribution to the middle game would be to identify, protect, facilitate, and support potential leaders from among all the people who were building the myriad processes and systems to create the sustainable business.

Several aspects of the middle game had implications I did not sufficiently anticipate, and are worth exploring further. I will address three: executive role conflict, the complexity of "going mainstream," and the impact of a severe industry downturn.

Executive Role Conflict. In hindsight, as we moved into the middle game, we were moving into a time when I should have expected role confusion among the leadership team. My opening charter of "eLearning," meant that my explicit authority did not actually extend over all the mainstream outcomes I claimed to be leading—product improvement, process development, partnership growth, and customer engagement. I had authority over some aspects of some of these arenas, but the authority for all of these arenas was distributed among my peers in marketing, sales, engineering, operations, and business development. Further, the potential for charter conflict was amplified by the simple fact that we had more executives on the team by the middle game. We had hired several more directors and, through the acquisition, gained another set of very talented executives with strong, relevant, and exciting experience in the industry. While I had a legitimate influencing leadership role for the overall transformation, the "real" charter for coordinating the middle game shifted upward to my boss, and the game itself became a much more collective activity. Even though we had all worked diligently and explicitly to this end, the shift in leadership roles necessary was not starkly clear to me at the time. We should have started working on specific role specification for the middle game sooner.

In retrospect, I believe this is a normal part of the middle game in this kind of transformation. We had a whole new team of executives and employees who only knew the new combined and repositioned business. For them, the opening game—when I was painstakingly building my team of change agents and coalitions—was ancient, unknown, and **irrelevant** history. They entered the game in the middle. People who were the original change agents for the opening game became a legacy the new executives did not understand. The job descriptions and roles that had sufficed to explain the eLearning team for the first year no longer worked, and this role conflict was not limited to me. It was much more panoramic. We faced questions like, "Why isn't this in marketing?" "Why isn't this in operations?" "Why is he in charge of that?" "What is her role?" The entire team of strong-willed, action-oriented executives and individual contributors was coming to grips with and trying to design the new organization at the same time we were all under the pressure to build the new business as quickly as possible.

The complexity of "going mainstream." The need to manage the transition from the provisional organization to a mainstream educational services organization required much more effort, planning, and resources than I anticipated. The middle game offered a classic Catch 22. The provisional eLearning team had the specialized and necessary knowledge, skill, and capabilities, while much of the mainstream educational services organization did not. Their skills and capabilities were in the traditional industry. Consequently, we could not abruptly transfer responsibility for fear that we would hurt our fragile eLearning business just as we were starting to build it. At the same time, the provisional team was much too small to support the business as the number of opportunities, complexity of the products and services, and installed base grew. We needed to keep a specialized eLearning team focused on building the business and at the same time, dissolve the specialized eLearning team so the mainstream marketing, sales, operations, and delivery teams could take over. At the start of the middle game, this tension was annoying, but not critical. But as the year wore on, the stresses and strains of organizational confusion became more pressing, and the need to dissolve my team became increasingly urgent. Given the clear difference between the opening and the middle game, I could have anticipated this issue.

Impact of an industry downturn. The severity of the industry downturn was an unpredictable influence on the middle game. I expected a shakeout in the eLearning industry, and it came exactly as we anticipated. And, like most people I realized that the "dot.com" explosion would not continue forever. However, the suddenness, severity, and timing of the industry downturn caught all of us off guard. This had a significant impact on our middle game, and it continues to have a significant impact on our end game.

The industry downturn put severe financial pressure on IT companies, ours included. This pressure had two direct impacts on our middle game. On the cost side, we found it difficult to fund and resource our business-building activities. Discretionary spending became severely constrained and since many of the emerging business costs were new (hence not in an established budget), we were particularly hard hit. At the same time, pressure on the revenue side increased significantly. Expectations to deliver sales accelerated at a time when all industry sales were dropping abruptly. Due to the severity of the industry downturn, the constraints of the middle game changed and the pace suddenly became much more intense.

In many ways, this may be seen as part of a normal business cycle. Good times give way to bad and leaders have to cope. Nonetheless, in retrospect, and knowing that we were in the middle game, I believe we could have responded more aggressively. Had the industry downturn happened in the opening, we could have simply abandoned the game. Had it happened in our end game, we could have executed a more traditional business response. Coming, as it did, in the middle game posed particular problems. We had to become very creative to continue to build the sustainable business that the middle game required.

At the beginning of the middle game, we had a small customer set, an additional customer pipeline that came with the acquisition, and a second revision of our software product. By the end of the year, we had developed basic processes, had a third revision of the software product in multiple languages, had deployed support models, and established a worldwide sales and marketing team. We had several big, strategically important customer wins and a growing pipeline. Though we certainly had not solved all problems, we ended the year with a vastly more robust offer and organization than we started it.

We also completed a reorganization to bring eLearning into our business unit mainstream. At the beginning of the middle game, I had a direct worldwide team of 24, an extended team of perhaps 100, and a clear charter to lead eLearning. By the end of the middle game, I had a team of 5, an informal network, and a new charter to develop long-term strategy and intellectual capital for general innovation. Indeed, by the end of the middle game, we had come a long way to establishing the sustainable business.

The End Game

End games can be very long—sometimes longer than the opening and middle game together. . . it is probably the most difficult part of chess . . . Both sides, too, have more space to move about in, which often means that there is a wider choice of plans than there is in the middle game. This does not mean a wider choice of good plans: usually there is only one good plan in an ending.

The skills you need to know for the end game can be reduced to two:
 (a) Promoting a pawn
 (b) Mating with a small force.[24]

The end game offers yet another transition.[25] In the opening, we moved through well-known moves with clearly anticipated outcomes. In the middle, we followed a few well-known principals to gain incremental and sometimes subtle advantages. In the end game, we build on the reality that has emerged from the middle game. In chess, the goal for the end game remains the same as the earlier stages: checkmate of the opponent's king. For me, the goal likewise remains what I started with: for my business unit (and, ultimately, the corporation) to become an industry leader in the technology enhanced learning industry.

In the end game, I remain assigned to the Educational Services Business Unit (though as will be noted below, there are corporate reorganization activities afoot that make this statement somewhat ambiguous). I have direct authority for a "small force" of highly trained learning design specialists and a charter for industry evangelism, learning systems research and development, and driving innovation and standards across all learning products and services. Most of my authority is in the category of influencing. At the corporate level, we are pursuing significant strategic redefinition and reorganization in response to the macro-economic situation as well as the specific industry conditions in IT. We (as a corporation) are redefining all our business units (including Education Services) and determining how all the units will work together.

Given this very brief summary of the background conditions in which my end game is taking place, I will visit the chess metaphor one last time. As in all games, the situation provides both challenges and opportunities, advantages and threats, good days and bad. In the end game of chess, there are relatively few skills on which the player must rely. The skills are conceptually straightforward, but effective execution is notoriously difficult. At the higher levels of chess, the end game requires extreme focus and stamina as well as mastery over emotions. These qualities are also characteristic of leading organizational transformations.

---

24. Pritchard. p. 126
25. At the time of writing, the end game is on-going.

In my case, the end-game skills require engaging the broader corporation and supporting other leaders. In many ways, these are two sides to the same coin.

Engaging the broader corporation. Ultimately, of course, a small business unit in a large corporation cannot, by itself, become an industry leader. A truly strong position in any global market requires the combined capabilities and resources of the entire corporation. Thus, in our end game, it is necessary to execute what might be termed in this case "going mainstream, reprise." In the middle game, we had to take the eLearning (and the attendant IT learning infrastructure) business into the mainstream of the educational services business unit. In the end game, we have to take it into the mainstream of the whole corporation. Naturally, this means that understanding the context of the corporation's "mainstream" is critical, and in our case that context is changing significantly due to corporate reorganizing and refocusing initiatives.

Two of these changes in the corporate context make our end game easier. First, since the corporation is integrating among the various business units much more aggressively, there is general momentum for all business units to "go mainstream." Second, the corporation is developing strong initiatives to leverage intellectual capital across all business units and with our partners. This creates a strong "internal market" for eLearning and knowledge systems. Thus, internally within the corporation, there is an emerging interest and imperative for deploying knowledge development, sharing, and management technologies as well as human capital management systems (what "eLearning" has grown into). Consequently, there is a more broadly held intuitive appreciation for the potential value of the endeavor.

Further, changes in the eLearning marketplace add to the corporate appeal for a strong business capability in technology enhanced learning systems. As we anticipated at the outset (over three years ago), the industry shakeout has had predictable results. The numerous smaller "pureplay" competitors in the eLearning industry are being supplanted by significant and strategic moves of the largest IT companies into this space. Three years ago, to the untrained eye in our company, "eLearning" appeared to be of interest only for the educational services business unit. However, over the past several years, the widespread use of technology in corporate learning projects and the resulting IT-industry challenges (such as integrating knowledge systems into existing corporate IT infrastructures, developing new technologies to improve system effectiveness and security, new designs to embed training directly into products, and massive learning/knowledge system deployments) have attracted attention of most large IT companies. It is becoming clear that eLearning has grown into an arena of technology enhanced learning (and knowledge) that is of competitive importance for the corporation.

Certainly, the corporate and industry restructuring is not all advantageous to our end game. Expertise in this business arena and industry is not widely spread throughout the corporate executive ranks. Consequently, there is an on-going potential for misunderstanding and confusion. At the same time, there are other parts of the corporation that have actively pursued various initiatives in eLearning, so coordination and integration with various other projects that are more or less compatible with ours requires effort. Finally, as in all such corporate activities, the sheer turmoil of reorganization, friction of new processes, and challenges of overcoming inertia add to the task. In short, the leadership challenge viewed from the point of view of my transformation project requires that I seek both to influence the corporate changes and be influenced by them. I must now synchronize my project with the larger whole and this requires additional effort.

One more outcome of the corporate reorganization should be addressed in some detail because it is relatively common. For a variety of reasons my boss and his boss left the company soon after the "end game" began. Just as we needed to begin our push to engage the broader corporation, two of our major corporate leaders were gone. This was a stark reminder of the reality of leading organizational transformation. New corporate leaders could decide to exit this business before they even understood what it is about. In my case, however, the new Education Services senior VP not only understood the effort, he had been a key leader throughout the opening and middle games. He stepped into the role instantly and led his part of the end game effectively. He and I and the entire evolving executive team, participated heavily in developing the emerging corporate strategies and articulating the role that eLearning and our growing capability could offer the corporations' business. However, this is also a reminder of two qualities of end game leadership that

I believe are general. First, **regardless of how effective the leader is, events outside his or her control can easily cause failure.** Second, **every leader's success depends on other leaders.** This introduces the second major leadership activity in my end game.

Supporting and Enhancing Other Leaders. No company can become an important global force in a market segment because of one (or even a few) leaders. The firm must have a wide set of confident, competent, and focused leaders. The chess metaphor offers another, vivid lesson to make this point clear. "Promoting a pawn" means that if a pawn is moved across the board so that it reaches the other side, it is promoted to the status of any piece (usually the queen). It changes from a very restricted range of maneuverability and impact to the maneuverability and impact of the most powerful piece. The pawn is often scorned by novice chess players, but it is treasured by experts precisely because they know that in the end game, promoted pawns are often the key to victory. I have found this a profound metaphor for leadership and for the responsibility of a leader. Looking ahead several years to the end game and the role that emergent leaders **will** play is possibly the most important strategic role in leading organizational transformation. As I said above, I believe my most important contribution in the middle game was nurturing nascent leaders. In the end game, building on this latent power of other leaders becomes central.

Some of these leaders are former members of my direct and "dotted line" eLearning organization. The original team has now dispersed into product marketing, market research, consulting, worldwide delivery, web portal architecture, operations, engineering, and customer engagement. These are all people who worked very closely together for over two years, who helped craft and execute the early vision, and who have strong specialist technical understanding of the market and the business opportunity. They are now an important network of leaders for the eLearning transformation dispersed throughout the corporation, all playing their critical role in growing, extending, and improving this business. Also, there is an important set of leaders throughout the corporation who were not on my direct team, but have been my peers throughout the past three years. They have played important roles in their part of the transformation in engineering, finance, human resources, corporate strategy, business development.[26] This complex web of leaders (viewed as part of the original project to "get in the game, stay in the game, and become an industry leader") is, **except to me**, largely invisible. Making these leaders stronger and the network of leadership more connected has been my most important end-game leadership task.

Stamina and Focus in the End Game. It seems a very long time ago that we began the moves that opened the game. Along the way there have been many possible diversions and many reasons to quit. After three years and countless meetings, many of the specific activities that I must do remain the same. I still need to articulate the basic logic and great potential of the investment the corporation has made. For people new to the idea, I have to continue to justify the effort and build awareness, push for innovation, and drive application. And I still have to routinely provide moral support to other leaders.[27]

> I do not think personal passion is enough to sustain leadership through the end game… Much of my stamina is merely a reflection of the stamina of the people I work with, and in some sense "lead."

Where does my stamina and focus come from after all these years? Certainly, I am passionate about the importance of this arena. I fervently believe that new designs for learning, knowledge, and human capital management systems (including technology, people, and processes) can change human organizations in ways that will improve the world. This basic passion is important. Without it, I could not have effectively led much beyond the opening. However, I do not think personal passion is enough to sustain leadership through the end game. At the start of this chapter, I said "Chess is a way to think about leadership without overstating the power of one leader or ignoring the fact that one person can make a powerful difference." Much of my stamina is merely a reflection of the stamina of the people I work with, and in some sense "lead." These people provide the energy,

---

26. I already mentioned the current senior vice president for Educational Services. He is a very important example of critical leadership, but only one of literally dozens of other leaders who are also critical to success. In general, the network of leadership is more important than any one of the leaders. However, at certain strategic points in the game, loss of one leader can certainly end the game.

27. Moral support is not one way. My peers and I joke that we take turns "talking each other off the ledge" depending on who has had the worst day.

both physical and emotional, to keep me going. On very difficult days, I am unceasingly motivated by the simple pressure of knowing that I cannot quit now that I have helped excite thousands—including employees, peers, partners, customers, industry analysts, and my bosses—to the cause.

Mastery Over Emotions. During the end game, there have been exceptionally exciting days, days when I was emotionally drained, and even some boring days. I suspect skilled chess masters face a similar set of emotional extremes during a typical end game. Some moves are simply playing out the obvious. Some moves are going for the win. Some moves suddenly reveal a significant threat. I have felt all these emotions (sometimes during a single day!) during our end game. A narrative like this always runs the risk of either overstating or understating the emotional aspects of leadership. In many papers on leadership, one is left with the impression that emotion plays no part for the leader. That is certainly not my experience. I will list only a few of the major sources of my emotional roller coaster.

First, of course, there is the constant possibility that something beyond my control will end the game quickly. Higher-level corporate decisions from a different business context always impact the context in which I am leading. Mergers, outsourcing, funding cuts, other corporate initiatives are all part of the constant backdrop for any business transformation in a corporate environment. The reality of uncontrollable, and often unpredictable, higher level decisions is not simply fear of game-ending possibilities. As often, the seeming caprice of corporate life provides good opportunities for this particular project. Rather, the main point is that a changing corporate context fuels an emotional roller coaster. The emotional impact comes from the lack of control and unpredictability as much as the potential negative impact.

Second, as has been described, much of leadership in the end game is work to strengthen and bolster other leaders in the organization. My contribution is often invisible and made manifest in the action, programs, and leadership of others. There are days when I would like to "get credit" for facilitating someone else's accomplishment. Armed, as I am with American-style individualist culture and models of leadership that focus almost exclusively on "leader as individual," my periodic craving for individual recognition is perhaps understandable. Certainly, the further reality that I exist in an employment environment where most explicit rewards are targeted at individual accomplishment adds to the mix. Indeed, one of the reasons that I value the chess metaphor so much is that it clarifies the importance of facilitating other leaders as a legitimate leadership contribution. It helps give voice to the importance of promoting the pawn.

The final source of the emotional roller coaster comes from my position at the nexus of the activities, which lets me see clearly the sheer enormity of the work that remains. My corporation and the technology-enhanced learning industry is changing rapidly. New technologies are being developed. Customers are increasingly sophisticated and demanding. New designs and standards are maturing rapidly. New partner patterns are emerging. New challenges boil up from our current engagements. New tools are needed. New processes must be created and implemented. New design metaphors must be crafted. More research is required. This is tremendously exciting, but on some days the scope of the challenge seems nearly overwhelming.

The End is a Beginning. At first, I thought I could not write this chapter since the end game is still being played and I do not know the result. We have certainly entered my long antic-ipated final step "to become an industry leader," but I cannot confirm success or failure. As has been true since the very first opening, every day offers the possi-bility that we will lose the game. However,

In the end, the chess metaphor breaks down, as must all metaphors. Unlike chess, in business as long as you have not clearly lost, the game never actually ends.

since my purpose here is not simply to report on my project, but rather to use the project to explore leadership through the chess metaphor, this is no disadvantage. In fact, the mere point that we have made it to the end game at all offered the possibility to explore the metaphor.

Various conventional metrics of business success (or shortfall) can be used to assess this kind of business transformation project. We have made significant sales and have a rich pipeline of opportunity, though not as strong as we would like. We are known and watched by influential industry shapers, although they are still skeptical about what we will do next. We have developed important intellectual property that can provide a basis on which we build for years, though we have not created industry-changing, breakthrough products. In the midst of significant corporate restructuring, the fundamental importance of our leadership position in the technology-enhanced learning industry is known and articulated by the highest level executives, though it certainly is not the most core activity for the corporation. In short, we have positive, but mixed, results.

In the end, the chess metaphor breaks down, as must all metaphors. Unlike chess, in business as long as you have not clearly lost, the game never actually ends. Though the metaphor punctuates critical transitions,

The end game of leadership does not end; it invites countless new openings.

highlights important points, and enables new ways to think about leadership, this difference is key. The end game of leadership does not end; it invites countless new openings. The end game—long anticipated, eagerly pursued, and where all the previous work can come to naught in a moment—is a draining endeavor requiring stamina, intense focus, and commitment. It lacks both the confident energy of the opening and the interesting creative engagement of the middle game. Yet, if you have been successful enough to reach it, the end game of business transformation is where you really win or lose. The end game is the daily grind of trying to lead the business to enhanced success.

Mike Wenger's interest in understanding the practice of leadership has been a common thread in his career. He retired from industry after over 30 years of varied experience, which included senior executive positions at Sun Microsystems (Worldwide senior director of Strategy and Innovation for Sun Knowledge Services, senior director of eLearning in Sun Educational Services), academe (teaching business strategy, international business, and entrepreneurship at Washington State University, the U.S. Air Force Academy, and Mercer University), and a successful private consulting practice focused on long-term strategy and change for clients in industry, government, and the non-profit sector. He also served over 20 years in the U.S. Air Force in leadership positions as both a pilot and on the faculty of the USAF Academy. Mike took his doctorate in international business and cross-cultural communication from Oxford University. He currently works with international humanitarian organizations in a variety of advisory roles. His interests include the use of technology to foster communication, coordination, and learning in and among organizations; innovation and change; and fostering education and business skills for humanitarian development. Mike is a long-standing friend of InterClass.

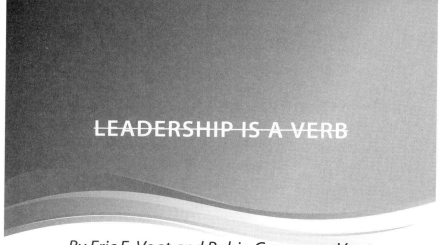

LEADERSHIP IS A VERB

By Eric E. Vogt and Robin Grumman-Vogt

Today leadership is clearly regarded as a verb, not a noun. This is demonstrated in the way that most corporations now describe their leadership development agenda by focusing upon leadership behaviors. Behaviors are the actions and reactions of our leaders in relationship to the environments in which they operate. Actions are verbs—hence, leadership is a verb. This is not news. But what is news, what appears to be changing, are the verbs that describe the leadership required to lead successfully into the future.

Leadership is a verb because leading has always required taking action and engaging others in taking action. Leadership is a verb because leading is a continuous process—a way of acting rather than simply a state of being. Having a "leader" title, a noun like CEO after your name, in today's world does not make you a leader. It is the actions in each moment that demonstrate who our leaders are. The best leader for one moment may not be the best leader for the next.

What verbs come to mind when we think of traditional leadership? Not long ago I think many would have listed verbs such as:

- command
- control
- direct

- delegate
- allocate
- monitor.

But increasingly today we operate with network leadership, that is, leadership where there is no continuously fixed leader. In network leadership, we are observing different people coming to the forefront as leaders under differing circumstances. Even titles like chairman of the Board no longer indicate an assured single-fixed point of leadership and direction. Stories from corporate boards and proxy fights demonstrate that leadership for change, even in large corporations, can come from the most unexpected places. The recent battle for control of the large European Bank, ABN AMRO, began with a two percent shareholder writing an open letter to the management about under-performance. Network leadership means that the person who takes the lead depends upon the characteristics of each specific situation—the expertise, depth of social network, the capacity to communicate, or availability required. These are unique capacities of individuals versus multiple styles of leadership that could possibly be enacted by one person. Linux, the operating system, offers one of the clearest examples of the right leader showing up at the right time. Bob Wolf and Philip Evans of BCG (Boston Consulting Group) in their Harvard Business Review article *Collaboration Rules* (July 1, 2005) discuss the mobile leadership of the ongoing maintenance and development of Linux. Linux is a free and open source operating system. This means Linux code is freely available to everyone and almost anyone can participate in projects and conversations about the future of Linux. The "father" of Linux, Linus Torvalds, and other long-standing members of the development network often function as final arbiters, but the raising of issues and opportunities to modify code and the validation of such issues and opportunities can and have come from the most unlikely places in the largely unpaid Linux developers network. Social characteristics of the Linux network demonstrate how particular people and their expertise get anointed to declare and work on particular coding problems or opportunities.

Social networks operate without hierarchical dimensions. Power resides in the strength of the ties of connection rather than the vertical levels of authority.

Not just at Linux, but everywhere, all our actions operate within social networks, the nexus of all the individuals with whom we interact. Social networks operate without hierarchical dimensions. Power resides in the strength of the ties of connection rather than the vertical levels of authority. Stronger ties and more trusting relationships connect us to the people with whom we interact most frequently. In a world run primarily by social networks, the verbs listed above, like command and control, will not get us where we need to go.

So, what are the key verbs of leadership in the 21st century? There are certain "basic" verbs required by almost all forms of work. These are:

- feel
- talk
- listen
- show
- think.

If we compare our list of basic "work" verbs to the old verbs, it would look something like this:

Feel   >>   Control

Talk   >>   Command

Listen   >>   Monitor

Show   >>   Direct, Delegate

Think   >>   Allocate, Control

Different basic verbs get more attention in different eras. When command and control forms of leadership were dominant, there was almost no emphasis on feeling or listening. Indeed, the command and control world was formed in the Industrial Age, where automation, repetition, and assembly lines dominated the process of adding economic value. It made sense in this world to characterize leadership in these terms. As the world grows more complex, it has become impossible for any one person to possess all the knowledge and styles of leading required to lead in every situation. Under these circumstances of increased complexity, listening and feeling have become more important. Listening as a leader means getting input from all parts of an organization or social system continuously. It is a powerful method to stay in touch with the changing needs of an organization, its markets, and its stakeholders. Leaders now are using what they hear and feel to enable the best individuals for each situation to lead.

While clear thinking is still an essential verb of leadership, we now also understand the importance of emotion in the cognitive process. The concept of emotional intelligence (EQ), popularized by Daniel Goleman, demonstrates the importance of taking into account emotional factors in decision making and other leadership actions. Goleman tells the chilling story of Patrick the red-headed pilot who became so angry when anything went wrong, that his co-pilots did not tell him about the fuel tank getting low. In this case, the plane went down with all aboard despite the fact that Patrick knew there was a back-up. Hopefully we can all learn from this negative leadership lesson and understand the value of an emotional climate that welcomes problems. And, as we will discuss shortly, the ability of leaders to sense and feel the emotional climate of the organization is more important today because structures of social and economic action are increasingly enabled by trust.

The verbs stressed in each era speak to the types of leadership required in that time. When the methods of "talking" are all about commanding, there is little space for the network leadership required by this new era. So what are the specific verbs that enable leaders to effectively feel, talk, listen, show and think in the 21st century?

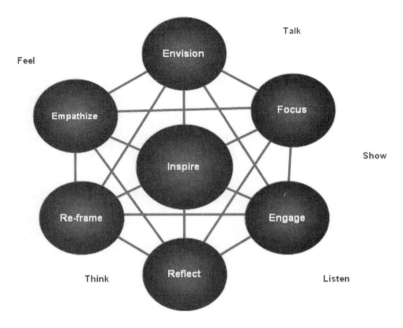

In the new era, the verbs that align with our basic "work" verbs have changed significantly. Many of the new verbs overlap the different categories established by the basic verbs, causing the new comparison to look something like this:

Feel   >>   Empathize, Inspire

Talk   >>   Focus, Inspire, Envision

Listen   >>   Engage, Reflect, Inspire

Show   >>   Focus, Engage, Envision

Think   >>   Reframe, Reflect

Feeling by new era leaders requires the "taking in" of the emotions of others in the form of empathy and the "giving out" of emotions for the purpose of inspiring others. This requires the use of verbiage that covers the emotional domain. Emotional verbiage includes deliberately asking questions about how people feel and not just what they think about their work, and having leaders match this with responses of their own that speak to how they feel about the work. But more subtly, the need for the presence of the emotional domain in organizations requires using words that connote emotionally inspiring conditions for an organization or team's specific work. For example:

- The new strategy will enable this organization to fulfill its destiny.

- The dogged loyalty of our workforce during economic downturns has enabled this organization to fare far better than its competition in difficult times and to leverage the advantages of the good times as a perfectly maintained machine.

AND

- Our people are the heart of our organization.

These three sentences are but a small example of the importance of images, stories, metaphors, and similes in fully expressing the emotional domain in the verbiage of leadership. The use of forms such as storytelling to tell a leader's authentic hopes and intentions offers enormous currency for generating inspiration in an organization. And, as we shall shortly discuss, inspiration is core to leadership in the new era.

Talking is very purposeful. How much time is spent talking is not an effective measure of leadership. In the new era, leaders talk for the purpose of focusing themselves and others. In the new era, leaders talk by asking powerful questions and listening for the insights of others. Focusing underscores priorities for immediate and long-term planning and action. Focusing inspires the realization of plans and is a key means for a leader to communicate what she envisions. Deliberate and planful repetition of key focusing statements is a core example of new era leaders using talking effectively.

Listening by leaders in the new era takes several steps. First, the leader engages others by inviting and inspiring them to present their views and needs. This is followed by reflecting on and articulating what has been heard. These two steps should follow one another as closely as time for reflection permits, in order for a leader to demonstrate that she has effectively heard others. Restating what has been heard in a leader's own words is a key method for new era leaders to demonstrate their listening.

Showing involves three verbs we have already encountered in other categories: engaging, focusing, and envisioning. But the meaning of these verbs is different in the context of showing. Here focus means to open the eyes of others to something previously unseen or unknown, while engaging refers to modeling engagement in the process or opportunity being shown. A prime example of leaders modeling engagement occurs when they show their passion for their organization and its mission and products. This ties to the reason for listing "envision" beside "show" in the diagram above. In this category, "envision" enables leaders to share their vision of how what is being shown fits into a broader context such as a strategy or mission. Steve Jobs' announcement of the iPhone, though directed as much at external customers as internal employees, is a superb example of a leader showing his passion, connecting it to an organization's mission and to the roles of its people—a connection that fosters engagement.

Thinking by new era leaders refers to the ability to reframe content, experience, and events to enable understanding and effective actions by others. Reframing enables a workforce to stay energized and mobile in the face of ongoing change and increasing complexity. Reflection enables leaders to develop and self-test reframes and develop perspectives on the issues and opportunities under their purview. Our society does value speed, but increasingly the quality of decision-making and other leadership processes takes precedence over immediacy or expediency. In short, there is increasing respect and understanding for taking time to think. On a large scale, we can see the power of re-framing at Apple. When Steve Jobs returned to the leadership position in 1997, he had a shrinking market share of the PC business and high costs to boot. By reframing Apple's destiny as the leading media company—music, images, videos—combined with Apple's legendary understanding of the computer-human interface, he and his team created a different company whose market cap exceeded Dell's in 2006. Also noteworthy is the significant improvement in *listening* Jobs achieved between his 1985 firing from Apple and his 1997 return to leadership. An advanced reframing skill is demonstrated when a leader reframes his own thinking and thereby changes his actions!

The ability to *inspire* defines the essence of leadership needed in the new era. As the diagram above indicates, the act of inspiring others is central to the leadership verbs for today and the near future. It would have been easy to make a case for the verb inspire appearing as an example in every one of the basic categories. Leadership has always involved the engagement of others, but today the incentives of pay and conventional social interactions—congeniality and affinity among co-workers—are not enough to inspire a workforce, whether paid or voluntary. Inspiration around a higher purpose is now essential. Organizations that match their higher purpose to the capabilities of the company and its products create strong engagement. Such is the case with Whirlpool, where in an alliance with Habitat for Humanity they donate their appliances to Habitat homes and offer Whirlpool employees time off to participate on site during home builds. Similarly, many corporations are now setting an objective of a sustainable environment, which is another acknowledgment of the importance of a higher-level purpose. This is not just a tip of the hat to "tree huggers," it is recognition that conditions like global warming impact all organizations and individuals. Business strategies around a sustainable environment foster good business, as they inspire employees and attract customers as well as new talent.

More and more today, societal changes and our legal system impel workers to become self-directed. By self-directed we mean that workers must increasingly look out for their own interests—this occurrence is very clearly demonstrated by the increasing use of employee-directed 401(K)s versus paternalistic company-controlled pension plans and increases in the number of workers who are freelancing. In the United States, about 80% of all workers either work offsite or work directly with people who do.[28] Inspiration is essential to coordinating action among a self-directed workforce. The ability to inspire is judged by its results. When acts of inspiration are successful, they generate commitment and initiate actions beyond what an individual would have achieved without external inspiration. Inspiration comes in many forms—appealing to a higher cause, or evoking the best abilities in each individual, or demonstrating the connectedness of today's assignment with the broader accomplishment it will enable in the future. Underpinning inspiration are the other verbs listed in the diagram, and all of them are empowered by trust.

Technique and technology are important, but adding TRUST is the issue of the decade.
—Tom Peters

Trust requires mutuality in our relationships—both give and take. The willingness to think and listen by reflecting on the words of others, as well as "talking" your own "envisionings," is essential to leadership for the future. Steven M.R. Covey has contributed to this field with his breakthrough book, *The Speed of Trust*. Steven points out that trust is not just nice to have, it is an essential ingredient of achieving effective, high-speed business transactions in a world where nanoseconds now matter. Leadership pundits such as Tom Peters have also identified trust as core to our success going forward. Covey quotes Peters as saying, "Technique and technology are important, but adding TRUST is the issue of the decade."

Reflection that leads to an accurate comprehension of the thoughts and needs of others is a trust enabler. Reflection is also a pre-requisite to trustfully creating reframes that enable leaders to move their organizations in a new direction. When a leader reframes her thoughts, her own "envisionings," to fit the needs of those she works with, she is able to move them to understand, agree to, and engage in coordinated action. The

---

28. Schaffner, H, and Van Horn, C., eds. (2003). *A Nation at Work: The Heldrich Guide to the American Workforce*. New Brunswick, NJ: Rutgers University Press.

outcome of coordinated action demonstrates a leader's ability to successfully inspire. When a leader is able to empathize—put herself in the shoes of other people—it enables the understanding that supports reframing to the needs of others' hearing. A leader who can present a view that both stretches ahead and stays focused will enable those she is leading to remain coordinated and inspired into the future. Again, simple restatements of what she has heard in a leader's own words along with the consistent repetition of key focusing statements are pre-conditions to successful reframes.

Trust is the currency of social networks and of inspiration. If I trust you, it is because you are

(1) **SINCERE**—I can believe what you say

(2) **COMPETENT**—you are able to do what you commit to

(3) **RELIABLE**—you consistently perform on your promises AND

(4) **COMMITTED** to the relationship—you demonstrate the effort required to maintain a trustful relationship—for example, you stay in touch (see Part II—Disengage to Engage for more on trust).

When all of these dimensions of trust are present I will welcome interacting with you within our shared social network and I am open to being inspired by you. Understanding the importance and the nature of the dimensions of trust is essential to leadership success in the new era. However, as the definition of trust above calls out, trust has multiple dimensions. Being conscious of how trust is built enables leaders to purposefully create trusting relationships, including curing breakdowns in particular dimensions of trust. The application of the new verbs of leadership can enable the demonstration of the various dimensions of trust.

Dimensions of Trust	Demonstrated By
Sincerity	Empathizing, Engaging
Competence	Reflecting, Reframing
Reliability	Consistent performance of all the 21st century leadership verbs
Commitment	Focus, Envisioning

Empathy is a powerful capacity. If you demonstrate, and not just express, empathy for my concerns and interests, I am assured of your sincerity. Empathy is demonstrated by a leader when she takes appropriate actions based on the validated understanding of the needs and concerns of others. To understand another's needs, a leader needs to *engage* with that individual or group versus assume understanding of their needs and thoughts. Competence can be well demonstrated with *reflection*. Leaders who seek out and reflect on new sources of input demonstrate a continuous drive towards increased competence or mastery. *Reframing* also demonstrates competence especially when it is based on careful past reflection.

Being conscious of how trust is built enables leaders to purposefully create trusting relationships.

Reliability is demonstrated by con*sistent behavior*. This form of trust can be engendered by consistently enacting all of the new era verbs of leadership. Commitment can be demonstrated by the presence of *focus* in a leader's own actions. Consistently being seen as focusing on one's publicly stated priorities engenders this form of trust. Commitment also relates to *envisioning* defined as follow through by leaders on their spoken visions for their organizations. Follow though develops trust that a leader is living commitments.

Leadership is a verb. Leadership is about action. The actions leaders take can build trust or destroy trust and where trust has been destroyed new actions can rebuild trust. Steven Covey, in his work "The Speed of Trust" has created a list of ten specific trust building actions leaders can take. We see each of these actions as offering an opportunity to develop one or more of the forms of trust. Being conscious about the dimensions of trust needs to be applied personally. Each leader, each individual, needs to consciously determine in which trust domains (sincerity, reliability, competence, or commitment) their own strengths and developmental opportunities exist. A leader who gets positive feedback on her sincerity, but is always late for meetings and deadlines, will be well served to work on reliability. It is important to continue to press forward on trust strengths while using techniques like those listed below to increase capacity where there are developmental opportunities. Leaders with self-knowledge can go far in heightening their trust levels within and beyond their organizations.

Trust Building Action	Form of Trust Enabled
Talk Straight	Sincerity
Create Transparency	Sincerity
Listen First	Competence (Reflecting)
Clarify Expectations	Competence
Keep Commitments	Commitment
Right Wrongs	Competence
Deliver Results	Reliability
Confront Reality	Sincerity, Competence & Reliability
Practice Accountability	Reliability
Show Loyalty	Commitment

Consistency in the performance of the actions described by Covey is required to build trust. This means that the opposite of the actions described must not present themselves often. Leaders can sometimes be blindsided by this. For example, keeping the day-to-day decision making of an organization transparent, but then having merger conversations in secret can often negatively impact the success of the eventually merged entity. Of course, there are times when the opposite actions may be necessary, sometimes loyalty has not been earned, for example, but conscious choice and appropriate communication are the essential ingredients to continuing to foster trust.

Even in the new era, there will still be times when verbs from a more hierarchical period such as command and monitor will still be required—just as they continue to be required in the armed services today. But even in the military, the increased attention now paid to the voices and leadership of many individuals—as in after action reviews[29] demonstrates how the presence of the new era leadership verbs we have described engenders the trust and the inspiration needed for successful innovation and change. "Leadership is a verb" may be generally understood. However, the key leadership verbs for this century have changed dramatically. We might all benefit by pasting these new verbs on our mirror, in order to reflect upon our effectiveness as leaders in this challenging century.

---

29. After Action Reviews (AAR) first formally developed by the U.S. Army, are structured de-brief processes that analyze what happened, why it happened, and how it can be done better in a forum that includes participants and those responsible for the project or exercise.

THE EQUANIMITY SHIFT OR, HOW TO LEARN OPTIMISM AND BE OPEN TO CHANCE

by Tom Cummings & Jim Keen

"If I could wish for something, I would wish for neither wealth nor power, but the passion of possibility; I would wish only for an eye which, eternally young, eternally burns with the longing to see possibility."

~ Søren Kierkegaard.[30] ~

Leaders are often praised for an aspect of their behaviour, as in, "she has always had charisma" or "he's an eternal optimist." In addition to what natural capabilities are possessed by such leaders, this chapter will give some attention to a 'starter pack' of practices that separately and collectively can be applied to develop more engaging and sustaining leadership. The practice that we want to explore is an attitude of mind, not a tool for the workplace. It is an attitude that must be developed, nurtured, and practiced. It is the idea of *equanimity*—an approach that underpins all that we advocate from our multi-year research project on how companies develop and sustain committed leaders. Equanimity may at first seem like an abstract notion, even a vague one, and it is in some sense elusive, but it is a vital dimension of optimal leadership.

---

30. Kierkegaard, Søren, et al. The Moment and Late Writings. Princeton U. Press.

The following thoughts are part of a larger work called Leadership Landscapes, to be published by Palgrave Macmillan, in 2007. We (Tom Cummings and Jim Keen) are the authors and creators of the Leadership Landscapes metaphor. This technique (and for some a way of life) is used by leaders to scan across multiple levels of a system and to expand their relational field of vision. It has been devised to create a backdrop and context for decision making and action taking. At the same time, the actions and decisions of leaders must also be informed by an attitude. For example, a leader may get to the right place on the landscape at the right time, but if their mind is not eagerly open to the potential that presents itself, the moment will be lost. Throughout this chapter we will come back to the dimensions of this 'right state of mind' called equanimity, or dynamic equilibrium.

The authors' view of equanimity comes from a quarter of a century of working with, interviewing, and studying exemplary leaders. One interview-based study, conducted over 15 years, revealed that leaders who sustain commitments to large-scale global and societal issues (such as public health, the environment, the prevention of deadly conflict and poverty) displayed a high degree of equanimity in their work on the organizational, team, and personal levels.[31]

With this study as our point of departure, we have spent the past decade working to refine our understanding of how great leaders work. Our exploration has yielded the keystone characteristic we call equanimity, which we can articulate as a balancing act—and one that those who have much to balance have a need to master. In common usage the term equanimity has come to mean "the quality of having an even mind" but it is much more.

It has become clear that equanimity is something that everyone has in some measure and that the measure of a person's equanimity can be increased through practice. Like a muscle in the body, a certain level of development happens by some combination of everyday use, exertion in meeting challenging circumstances and practices directly targeted at its development. Muscles tend to work in sets. In this sense equanimity is

---

31. Common Fire: Leading lives of Commitment in a Complex World. Laurent Parks Daloz, Cheryl H. Keen, James P. Keen, Sharon Daloz Parks. Beacon Press, 1996.

similar to an integrated muscle set with multiple applications and ways of working. Our favourite view of equanimity reveals an integrated set of attributes held together by a nucleus, in which each attribute is an expression of the whole characteristic. Of what then, is this set of attributes comprised?

An Eye for Possibility

The first attribute, the eye for possibility, resonates with the quote that heads this chapter. Equanimity is about being able to see possibility in the face of challenge, disappointment, adversity, and even despair. In his autobiographical account of the psychological degradation he saw daily and experienced himself in a Nazi concentration camp, psychiatrist Viktor Frankl relates how he discovered the elemental nature of meaning making.[32] In the second half of this book, which continues to speak to audiences today across more than a half century, Frankl describes the approach to addressing despair that emerged for him out of the ashes of the concentration camp. He tells the story of an older professional man who came to his psychiatric office one day, "Dr. Frankl," he announced, "since the death of my wife, I am unable to get on with my life. I loved her so deeply and my heart is broken from losing her." Frankl's approach was inquiry and his quest was to ask the question that would trigger his patients' shift from despair to possibility by which they would find for themselves a way to make new meaning out of their suffering. Frankl asked "what if you had died and left her to grieve?" The patient, as he considered this, saw a new possibility.

By surviving his wife and bearing the pain of her loss, he could act out of love for her, knowing that by surviving her, he had spared her the pain of losing him and having to get on with her life. The despair was lifted as he shifted to this possibility and he left Frankl cured of his despair.

When thinking about equanimity it seems best to regard it as a quality embodied in leaders rather than presented as a series of qualities *abstracted* from leadership. So for the purposes of exploring equanimity we will use exemplars drawn from the public stage of the past three-quarters of

---

32. Viktor E. Frankl. *Man's Search for Meaning*. Washington Square Press, 1984.

a century or so and illustrate how each shows an acute eye for possibility.

Nelson Mandela dedicated himself as a young adult to the struggle for equality in South Africa. He acted on this possibility during his lifetime as an adult, first through non-violent strategies that South Africans had learned from Gandhi, who led his first campaigns for the rights of Indians in that country. Then, after the advent of apartheid, when it became clear that the government had little hesitation about firing on non-violent protestors, he broke with the tradition of his political party, the African National Congress (ANC) and led a movement to train saboteurs for action against military and government targets, "always taking care for life and limb," as he reports in his autobiography.[33] For this initiative he became an outlaw and was eventually captured and convicted of several capital crimes. At his trial he closed his statement, famously, with the words: "During my lifetime I have dedicated myself to this struggle of the African people. I have fought against white domination, and I have fought against black domination. I have cherished the ideal of a democratic and free society in which all persons live together in harmony and with equal opportunities. It is an ideal which I hope to live for and to achieve. But if needs be, it is an ideal for which I am prepared to die."[34]

The possibility for which Mandela dedicated his life was realized through a global movement that initiated internal and external campaigns to put pressure on the white business community, a key constituency of the National Party, to force the abandonment of apartheid. By the end the 1980s, the campaigns yielded fruit as a new set of National Party leaders who had grasped the end of apartheid as not only a possibility but as a political necessity, came to power. In 1990 Mandela was released from his life term in prison and in leading the ANC to abandon the threat of violence, initiated a movement toward national reconciliation that culminated, in 1994, with his election as president of the country in the first universal democratic election ever held there.

Nelson Mandela's eye for possibility kept him moving through a lifetime of commitment. For him there was the "enduring ideal of a

---

33. Nelson Mandela. *Long Walk to Freedom*. Macdonald Purnell, 1995.
34. http://www.anc.org.za/ancdocs/history/mandela/1960s/rivonia.html.

democratic and free society in which all persons live together in harmony and with equal opportunities." And throughout his life of leadership he found possibility after possibility to move toward that ideal. While ideals, like horizons, almost always elude complete realization, in the end, it is our long walk toward them that fires our commitment. An acute eye for possibility, like Mandela's, recognizes the silver lining against the background of the cloud and, when seeing the glass, looks to both how it is half full and how it is half empty—the possibility highlighted as foreground in relation to the background, the landscape, the knot of problems that possibility addresses. This is what illuminates a leader's vision of the way opening toward the horizon.

Enduring Commitment

Our second exemplar is a woman who has not yet realized her aim but has become a beacon of possibility for her nation and a for her nation's possibility to the world. Aung San Suu Kyi is the daughter of Burma's most respected independence hero, Aung San, who was assassinated in 1947, the year before the end of British colonial rule. She returned to her native country, by then for 26 years a military dictatorship, from England in 1988, to be at the side of her ailing mother. Inspired by the democracy movement she found sweeping across the country and in the direct aftermath of the military firing upon and killing thousands of democracy demonstrators, she sent an open letter to the government asking for the formation of an independent People's Consultative Committee to prepare for multi-party elections. On the 26th of August 1988, she addressed a rally of 500,000 people gathered in front of the Shwedagon Pagoda in Rangoon: "I could not, as my father's daughter, remain indifferent to all that was going on."[35]

As we write, she continues to lead this struggle despite being placed under house arrest in 1989. In 1990, a reorganized military dictatorship allowed multi-party elections. The National League for Democracy (NLD), with Aung San Suu Kyi as secretary general, won 82% of the seats contested. "The military regime ignored the results, refused to allow the

---

35. http://www.moreorless.au.com/heroes/suukyi.html.

parliament to convene and jailed the NLD's elected candidates."

Now, more than a decade later, after numerous episodes of house arrest and release, yet a third reconfigured military government continues to rule the country. Aung San Suu Kyi continues to symbolize opposition to them, consistently inviting dialogue, advocating non-violent resistance, calling for an increasingly complacent international community to care about her imprisoned country, and pointing to the possibility of a democratic future for her fellow citizens. Like Mandela she is a leader who points always toward possibilities, toward a horizontal vision with her very life. She has indeed succeeded many times over in demonstrating the illegitimacy of a government that has impoverished its own people. Whether the light of possibility that she shines against the dark background of dictatorship will cause the military regime to give way in the end, is anyone's guess. Yet her heroic leadership remains the symbol of the Burmese people's struggle for freedom.

A third leader, whom many people would acknowledge as the world's leading exemplar of equanimity is the Dalai Lama. A global religious leader to be sure, he is also the temporal leader of the Tibetan people. The Dalai Lama, whom each of the authors has met in separate situations, sometimes reflects on coming to grips with his anger at the Chinese invasion of his homeland, which China claims as its own, and the treatment by the Chinese of the Tibetan people. Many now live, as he does, in exile and the remainder are now outnumbered in their homeland by Chinese who have immigrated there with the backing of the Chinese government. The Dalai Lama emphasizes compassion for all sentient beings including his Chinese adversaries on every occasion. He has spent his life looking for a possible reconciliation with the Chinese and for new possibilities for his leadership of his people. For his efforts he has, like Nelson Mandela and Aung San Suu Kyi, been awarded the Nobel Peace Prize and continues to draw hope for a return to his homeland from witnessing the end of the Soviet domination in Eastern Europe, something few had predicted as occurring in the years and even months before the velvet revolutions and toppling of the Berlin Wall in 1989.

The Dalai Lama's eye for possibility has led him to rebuild the seat of his temporal leadership of Tibet's government in exile in Dharamasala, India, which has now become a thriving centre for the perpetuation of

Tibetan culture. Moreover he has become an iconic leader in the pursuit of peace and compassion throughout the world. As a world figure, he has championed the possibility of fruitful encounter between and among the world's religions. His is as great and as wide-ranging an eye for possibility and for leading others in the pursuit of possibility, as can be found among leaders in the contemporary world.

Our final exemplar of possibility is one who long ago passed from the world stage, yet remains one of the more profiled and most respected leaders of the 20th century for his role as one of the leaders of the allies in defeating the axis powers in World War II, and for envisioning the establishment of the United Nations. Franklin D. Roosevelt was affable, liked to live the good life and aspired to political office as a Democrat. After serving as assistant secretary of the Navy under Woodrow Wilson he became the Democrat's nominee for vice president in a contest the Republicans were heavily favoured to win. After losing this contest, Roosevelt was struck down in 1921 with a devastating disease that caused his permanent paralysis from the waist down that lasted the remainder of his life.

Ability to Meet New Situations

It was in the face of this adversity and as a result of his struggle to regain the ability to walk, that Roosevelt appears to have developed a fresh eye for possibility. It was a long haul, five years of frustration when, in 1926, he purchased the rundown health spa in Warm Springs, Georgia, where he had gone earlier to seek recovery. It was in this context that he learned to simulate walking with the help of braces by shifting his body from side to side as he used his upper body to propel himself with canes. His success in the face of physical handicap was enough to convince his party's political operatives that he could make a comeback, as he eventually did, by being elected two years later to the governorship of New York.

His eye for possibility served him well in his run for the American presidency in 1932 when he promised government action to address the economic malaise into which the country had fallen. He soon followed up with an activist agenda that fuelled the growth of government and brought extraordinary power to the presidency. A pragmatist by nature, he would try anything he thought might work, and some of his initiatives during the 1930s met with more success than others.

Much more important than Roosevelt's economic achievements were his abilities to project himself as leader and marshal the forces of government into action. From his days of self-propelled rehabilitation, he developed an attitude of determination to meet any situation that presented itself.

In exemplary leadership, the eye for possibility makes the greatest difference when it seeks opportunities to express its beholder's enduring commitments. And each of our exemplars displayed endurance over a considerable period of time. This idea of durability in the face of adversity is the second expression of equanimity that we have found to be vital.

As we have seen, Nelson Mandela was enduringly committed to a free multiracial democratic society of equal opportunity. That was his commitment on the societal landscape. On the political landscape he was equally committed to the African National Congress as the organizational means to wage the struggle for freedom within the political arena. At the level of his own leadership he was deeply committed both to a pragmatic search for what would work and to a moral compass that brought great dignity to his leadership. At the Rivonia trial, Mandela explained:

> At the beginning of June 1961, after long and anxious assessment of the South African situation, I and some colleagues came to the conclusion that as violence in this country was inevitable, it would be wrong and unrealistic for African leaders to continue preaching peace and non-violence at a time when the government met our peaceful demands with force. It was only when all else had failed, when all channels of peaceful protest had been barred to us, that the decision was made to embark on violent forms of political struggle, and to form *Umkhonto we Sizwe*...the Government had left us no other choice.

That he had never advocated a terror campaign targeted at civilians made it possible, when the moment came, for Mandela to trade the tactic and threat of violence for the principle and actuality of a South Africa in which all adult citizens would cast votes of equal weight regardless of their color or status. From there, his moral compass led him to leadership of a unity government, to work toward reconciliation of the nation's ethnic groups and ultimately to the greatest legacy that he, as the first fully democratically elected leader of his country, could leave to his fellow citizens—to step down from the presidency at the end of his elected term.

Our earlier profile of Auug San Suu Kyi points directly to her deep commitments to the future of her people and to the leadership of the party that won the right to govern in a landslide vote and was denied by an arrogant military junta who mistakenly thought they would win and therefore gain the legitimacy that they continue to lack. At the deepest level her commitment to the non-violent principles of Burmese Buddhism underpins her endurance and tells her to seek dialogue and reconciliation as a means to end military rule. But her repeated acts of dignified disobedience continue to uphold the possibility of a different future for the Burmese people and to reflect the profound misrule of the military oligarchy to the rest of the world.

Roosevelt's commitments were large in scope, first overcoming the Great Depression, later, as one of the leaders taking the allies to victory in World War II and, pointing toward the horizon to a post-war world with a robust United Nations keeping the peace and addressing the end of colonial empires. He tended to be flexible and pragmatic about the means to these ends.

His mediation of the several landscapes of wartime is caught by the following vignette. "I am responsible," Roosevelt once told (General) George C. Marshall during an argument over strategy, "for keeping the grand alliance together. You cannot, in the interest of a more vigorous prosecution of the war, break up the alliance" (which was necessary to win the war).[36]

Being Present and Projecting Presence

The third aspect of equanimity is presence. Colleagues of ours who run a consulting firm, speak of presence in terms of the influence you

---

36. David Stafford. *Roosevelt and Churchill Men of Secrets*. Overlook Press: 2000.

have when you walk into the room and of how leaders cast their shadow on their team. Is it energizing, neutral, or deflating to be in their presence? Our attention to presence has been long standing as we have been influenced by the philosopher and activist Douglas Steere and his 1966 publication *On Being Present Where You Are*.[37] Steere's approach is one that could be used as a bedrock for equanimity. He lists four qualities that are worth lodging as we explore leadership and equanimity. These are: first, the importance of being vulnerable (open), the second is acceptance (of our ability to change what we can but that there are some things we cannot influence), the third is expectancy, and the fourth is constancy.

The Latin and Greek origins of the word constancy mean to "stand with" or "stay with" another. Steere speaks of "infinite patience." Really to listen to another, you have to exercise true patience. Finally from Steere, it is worth noting that, and in common with many of the world religions, little distinction is made between being a servant and being a leader, the same qualities are required.

In *Common Fire*[38] (a book co-authored by one of us) there is an excellent illustration of the quality presence to which Steere speaks. The dean of a graduate school, widely admired for the broad commitments and achievements that distinguished his career, reflected in an interview on significant influences in his life. An African American veteran of World War II, he found himself in graduate school at an Ivy League University, where he was very much a minority. There he had as his mentor a widely known and respected scholar—the jewel in the crown of that graduate faculty. The interview spoke of the many struggles he faced during that time and how he would look forward to his meetings with this professor.

> You would enter his office and sit down at the appointed time and he would be deeply into his scholarship, reading, sometimes writing. Then when he turned toward you, you felt his full presence inviting you to share with him whatever you needed to communicate about your scholarly work or about other life circumstances affecting your performance.

37. On Being Present Where You Are, Douglas V. Steere, Pendle Hill Pamphlet 151
38. Common Fire: Leading Lives of Commitment in a Complex World, Laurent Parks Daloz, Cheryl H. Keen, James P. Keen, Sharon Daloz Parks, Beacon Press, 1996

And he would listen carefully and respond constructively to all you shared. And I have made it a point to carry that forth in my own work. To come as close to that full presence as I can as often as I can.

Presence, then, is about how we show up, how we listen, and how we cast our shadow. We have developed a way of thinking about presence that brings together two qualities: authenticity and appropriateness. In order for leaders to be fully present where they are (in Steere's terms) and to cast a constructive shadow (in the McLean terminology) they have to find their voice in a way that is both authentic to themselves and appropriate to the situation in which they find themselves.

Our exemplars clearly exhibit this kind of presence both in the flesh and in how they project themselves as leaders. Mandela's presence in the courtroom in his statement and demeanour before being sentenced to a life prison term held his place in the political arena. Most remarkable was the presence that this statement helped him to continue to project as his words echoed ever more sharply against the silence over more than 20 years of absence from the stage of politics. Moreover, when he emerged from prison his presence in the flesh stood up to what he had projected with his words years earlier as he worked tirelessly to achieve the transition to a multiracial democracy. To study Mandela is to study a record of presence spanning at least half a century.

Like Mandela, Auug San Suu Kyi projects presence even as her adversaries try to hide her from view in isolation or house arrest. She presents a dilemma for her captors. If they harm her, they risk increasing the millions of small acts of resistance by a people who already move a bit more slowly, produce a little less, keep their own secrets, all of which tend to dampen the rule of brutal authoritarian regimes. If they let her go free they know she will not be quiet and will continue to call upon them to restore democratic rule. In the end, this is an unarmed woman holding the mirror of oppression up to a band of dictators who are armed to the teeth. As the world notices, she projects her presence.

The Dalai Lama exudes presence when he addresses an audience, large or small, in the flesh. He is, to say it simply, one of the best known and widely recognized leaders in the world today. But like Auug San Suu

Kyi and Nelson Mandela, he projects his presence on behalf of two causes. One is the fate of the Tibetan people. The other is the cause of compassion. If not for his presence, which is due primarily to his having become the world's most visible and persistent advocate for compassion, the plight of the Tibetans would by now have slipped way beneath the radar of the world press, a fait accompli of little consequence.

Roosevelt could be a textbook case for projecting presence. His 1933 inaugural speech projected a sentiment that was authentically him, true to his own experience, and quintessentially appropriate to the moment. He addressed a people about a third of whom were out of work and facing destitution and many others who feared they might not be far behind. That speech is best remembered for its keynote words, "We have nothing to fear but fear itself." It rang true because it captured the behaviour of panic that fuelled the downward spiral of deflation. It also spoke to the courageous government actions he felt necessary to restore the economy while inviting his fellow citizens to join him in the courageous spirit with which he intended to lead. And once he had captured the imagination of his constituency, and he continued to hold it through a series of "fire side chats" that he delivered throughout his presidency. He created at once a sense of intimacy and of high purpose aimed at enlisting his fellow citizens in the project of nation rebuilding.

Flexible Reframing

Allied to this ability to hold presence is the art of deftly reframing a situation or set of challenges, which in turn is also dependent on an ability to see possibility when others see none. This is the fifth element of equanimity. To shift one's frame is often as much a matter of changing the background in front of which a figure is set as it is a matter of changing how the figure is set against the background. Which way it is done matters less than finding a fresh approach to dealing with a problem set or a different way forward for a previously intractable situation.

This contrasts, of course, with the all too frequent leadership gambit, which amounts to this: if your approach is not working, do more of it or do it harder. While this sometimes can yield results—often enough to reinforce the leader into repeating their behaviour—it is a costly leadership strategy particularly when it becomes habitual, that can yield leadership burnout, team failure, and organization dysfunction.

Sustained leadership in pursuit of enduring commitment almost always includes short-term reframing at the level of immediate intent, which should be practiced with ease or even without thinking about it. Deeper levels of intent require deeper thought and a reframing of enduring commitments that generally bespeak some form of transition in leadership or life. While all of these may be associated with equanimity, it is the relatively instant and flexible reframing that we associate most strongly with the term.

Flexible reframing relates strongly with the readiness to face a new situation, where finding suitable frameworks for sense-making is often required immediately, and, in the case of exemplary leaders, the reframing process is used repeatedly to tune themselves more acutely to the situation as it evolves. There is also an interesting relationship between flexible reframing and enduring commitment.

Recovering Oneself

The sixth and final attribute of equanimity resides in the capacity to bounce back or recover oneself. Remember how Roosevelt overcame his crippling disease? How he overcame his defeat as vice president? His indefatigability was displayed again during his wartime leadership and in the final months of his life when his health was clearly failing.

Coming back or returning to equanimity can be like facing a new situation because equanimity is either maintained or momentarily lost and then recovered. In facing a new situation there is always the possibility of being knocked askew by the force of circumstance, but returning to equanimity is always about getting back to balance—it is about recovering oneself so that one stands in confidence, performing in an optimal manner.

The recovery of equanimity or one's sense of balance in the wake of losing it in a challenging situation can be likened to the manner in which an athlete gains, regains, and maintains balance in the flow of performance. It is done kinaesthetically, by being in tune with the body's balancing mechanism—a dance between the inner ear, body memory from training and a flow of quick, precise decisions in the interface of the conscious and subliminal mind. So it is with recovery of equanimity. There appears to be some kind of trigger, something akin to the inner ear in physical balance, and some form of letting go of what is holding one out of balance, that shifts one back into balance. So how do leaders stay in dynamic balance?

This brings us back to our starting point. Earlier we described equanimity as an integrated set of attributes held together by a nucleus. We see that nucleus as the balancing point of the mind. Equanimity is often defined in a manner that comes close to this understanding when it is defined as "even-mindedness." We prefer a more robust but compatible expression—dynamic equilibrium—the sense of maintaining balance in the flow of thought and action and triggering a return to balance when it has been disrupted.

Let's go back to this issue of triggering the shift back to equanimity—to dynamic equilibrium or, if you will, to even-mindedness. Think back to our earlier example of Viktor Frankl's questions through which he aimed to trigger a shift for his clients from misery, despair or the numbness of not caring back to a fresh possibility for moving forward in their lives without ignoring, shrouding, or burying the problem that was troubling them. What Frankl would trigger is what healthy minds often learn to trigger within themselves.

So it is with equanimity. Leaders who sustain enduring commitments and keep themselves robust and flexible in facing an uncertain, changing world of multiple landscapes, have either learned how to trigger their own rebalancing reflexively or have learned to trigger rebalancing more consciously through means they can access when they sense the loss of balance. There are a number of means for doing this and the best advice may be to locate the triggers for rebalancing that one uses naturally and learn to trip them more consciously.

Finally, we come to a presentation of our relational map of equanimity, which configures so as to incorporate the six attributes, each one to the other five. Notice that we place the balancing point—the dynamic equilibrium—at the centre as the nucleus that pulls the frame together. Each attribute can be seen as an area of focus or attention that if practiced, over time, will lead to leadership readiness and mastery. In this way, we enter into a new perspective on leadership that moves away from the notion of 'inborn attributes' and 'situational responses' to the practice of a new set of leadership abilities—a shift to equanimity—across the landscapes of one's work and life.

The Relational Integrated Framework of Equanimity (RIFE) as in rife with possibility

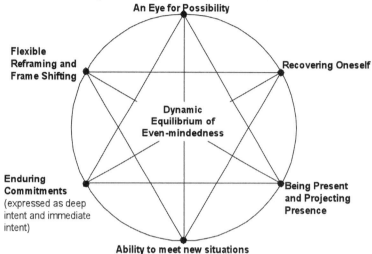

Tom Cummings

Tom Cummings is a co-founder and partner of Executive Learning Partnership (ELP). He has served as the head of learning and organization for Unilever and ABN Amro Bank, was an academic at IMD International in Lausanne, Switzerland and today he is the associate director of the New Board Program at Nyenrode University where he lectures on leadership and governance.

Tom is a board member of Common Purpose Netherlands and collaborates with Charles and Liz Handy to develop leaders through the Tällberg Forum in Sweden.

Tom has co-authored the book *Leadership Landscapes: how Leaders sustain dynamic balance in a complex world*, published in December 2007, Palgrave MacMillan Press.

Tom is a long time friend of InterClass and served as a member of the Advisory Council when he was the head of learning at Unilever.

Jim Keen

Jim Keen (James P. Keen) has been coaching for more than thirty years serving leaders from business, government, the non-profit sector, and higher education. Keen earned his doctorate from Harvard University where he also administered the Interdisciplinary Committee on International Studies in the Faculty of Arts and Sciences. He has held teaching appointments at Harvard and several other universities. At Monmouth University he was the first incumbent of The Millicent Fenwick Distinguished Chair. He also served as vice president and dean of Antioch College, as founding executive director of the Governor's School of New Jersey, as chairman of the board of The International Center for Integrative Studies and as senior research scholar at The Bonner Foundation. Keen is co-author of *Leadership Landscapes* and of *Common Fire: Leading Lives of Commitment in a Complex World*.

TALENT: THE LOST CHILD

By Evelyn Taylor

Global Organization Development Manager, Reed Elsevier

The views expressed by the author are her own and not those of Reed Elsevier, Inc.

So much has been written recently about the topic of talent that it's accumulating an array of new aliases: "Talent Management," "Talentship," "Valuing People," "People Development," and the like. A lot of people are talking about talent these days, too. Thousands of speeches, workshops, conferences, teleclasses, and executive retreats are offered yearly on the topic. Our universities are making talent a *Talent is People!* key business niche by expanding the number of executive development programs focused on the latest trends in coaching and other areas related to talent. But what exactly do we mean by "talent?" Is it just the latest term for "employees," or even more simply, "people?" In this chapter, I will attempt to describe and define "talent" and what it should mean to leaders going forward.

While you may not be among those actively seeking the lastest strategies and theories about talent, it's likely you have come face to face with the topic while sipping your favorite latté at a neighborhood café. It happened to me not too long ago while getting my caffeine fix and browsing my top 10 magazine picks. There in the stacks, yelling out to me, was the cover article of *Fast Company*'s August 2005 issue: "Why We Hate HR."

Having been an HR professional for the last…well, never mind how many years, I was intrigued and sat down in my favorite cushy chair to read just why it is that people in my function are despised. Although humorous and enlightening, the article left me further convinced of something I had been thinking and talking a lot about lately. Despite the apparent increased energy in the atmosphere around talent, the fact of the matter is, no one seems to be responsible for it. Talent is a lost child.

Consider this: if you are fortunate enough to be working in the most important function in an organization, which is HR (okay, I had to get that in), think back on how many times you've gone head-to-head with a line manager who wasn't devoting adequate attention to what is most important—that is, to PEOPLE. How many times have you made excuses to a candidate, because when you went into the office of the vice president you were greeted with rolling eyes and instructed to make the appointment go away? Have you had the pleasure of informing a director that it was time for performance conversations with his or her staff, only to hear the moans and groans associated with this dreaded task? Or perhaps, at annual budget preparation time, you've heard managers insist that the only way to make year-end targets is to downsize, cut heads, reduce headcount? Whatever term you use, all too often cutting staff is a shortsighted action because, as many of us have seen, troops are rehired at that magical moment when the budget turbulence calms down. Of course, we don't hire the same troops and the new ones don't know what the fired ones did, so we start the whole learning cycle over again.

Okay, I think I may be hitting a nerve, because I believe at some point many of us have lived these experiences—or as my nephew would say, *Been There, Done That!* While life in HR does differ from one organization to another, I do think my HR colleagues would agree on a few fundamental truths:

- First of all, as HR professionals we tend to spend too much time pushing initiatives and solutions that are supposed to help people feel valued and appreciated, but don't.

- Secondly, these "solutions" will never work because at the crux of this whole talent issue is one **key point:** If managers of people don't genuinely and sincerely believe that the success and sustainability of their divisions, organizations, and companies is due to their PEOPLE (not talent), then all of these HR actions are worthless.

- Finally, there should not be "HR" actions—there should be principles and values that are integral to the way leaders run businesses!

So what does this all mean? To me it is clear—the lost child must be given a home. Accountability for talent must move from HR to line and board responsibility. Line leaders must assume responsibility and elevate the priority and focus on people—finding, keeping, and developing the right people must be viewed as **the** most influential determinant in whether your business thrives or dies. And this priority on people should go even further up the food chain—it should be a primary area of focus for the board of directors. If a board's role is to oversee how an organization operates and provide advice accordingly, then the board should take an active, ongoing interest in the organization's people and make every effort to ensure the right people are in place to make the organization soar.

Line leaders need to move some important "people" questions to the forefront of their minds and put them on the agenda of those power meetings. These are the topics of leadership; they need to be discussed, debated, and wrestled with at the leadership table.

Speaking of this infamous table, it strikes me that HR is often conspicuously absent, which in turn makes me think that organizations often behave like dysfunctional families. At our crazy Irish family gatherings there is the power table where my mother sits with the "elders," and the not-so-important folding TV tables where screaming nieces, nephews, and other "outcasts" are seated. If you arrive late or if you have said something to anger or annoy the elders, to the TV tables you go! I would argue that in many organizations, HR is not invited to the leadership table because leaders don't want to answer the questions (like the ones in the next section) raised by good, courageous HR people!

Given that 2006 was the year when the hippies of yesterday (baby boomers) began exiting for retirement, leaders should ask themselves:

- Who am I worried about losing?

- Who has built those essential relationships (with customers, in the community, with employees) that are so priceless and vital that losing this person will put our organization at a signifcant disdavantage?
- What key experiences and know-how will no longer be here, and, more importantly, what have I done to make sure the void is addressed?
- As I think about replacements for these priceless gems, how much effort do I extend?
- Do I wrestle with these decisions or simply move deck chairs?
- How confident am I that we are putting the right people in the right slots?

And if leaders truly care about cutting-edge ideas and continuous innovation (as they say they do), then I'd suggest they ask themselves:

- As I look out over the cubicles, desks, and offices in this company, how confident am I that the next breakthrough idea is in the hearts and heads of the people I employ?
- If we say we are all about innovation, do I relentlessly puruse individuals who are "out there" and how will these people fit into this organization and its culture?
- Do I reward people for producing the most predictable or most innovative results?
- Who will provide the ideas that will make this company thrive, keep us honest in everything we do, and allow us to fulfill what we dreamed of doing?
- What disasters have occurred that we didn't foresee, and which ones could happpen in the future? If they did occur, could my troops rise to the occasion? If not, what's missing?

Since leadership starts within, leaders need to look in the mirror and ask themselves:

- Do I send mixed messages by my actions? For example, if faced with a manager who really brings in the bucks and powerful clients but is brutal to work for and with, what action do I take?

- Am I tolerating mediocrity by having my pals versus the best people for the organization?
- Do I shy away from the tough conversations that make your stomach churn but need to be held?
- What do I really care about and stand for, and is this clear to the organization?
- Am I authentic?
- What do I want this organization to be? What do we stand for? What are our values?
- What kind of people do we need to achieve this? Do I have them?
- If not, what do I need to do to get them and keep them?

When clear answers to questions such as, "What kind of people do we need"? do not exist, then an organization is operating without a solid, sustainable foundation. The absense of answers to questions like these indicate basic gaps in our explicit understanding if the nature of our organizations, products, and processes.

After these larger questions are answered by leaders, we first need to start thinking about the next level of questions to determine what HR-specific processes make sense. HR should be about helping the organization develop a means to frame these questions, a process for grappling with them, and a system of appropriate responses.

- What makes sense in terms of people based on how this place is organized?
- What is really rewarded, and what is punished?
- What will make people thrive, and what will aggravate them?
- What will ensure that values are truly the words we live by rather than the words we espouse?
- What talents and skills will make us soar?
- What behaviors will ruin us?
- What do I need to stop doing? Do differently?
- What do I need to create?

Straight questions and accurate, courageous answers are what's needed, but the questions need to emanate from the person running the organization, not from HR. People need to be first and foremost among the organization's priorities, rather than an afterthought, which, unfortunately, is often the norm. Shifting people from an HR responsibility to a business leader priority is the change that must happen now.

Leaders own responsbility for these questions, but they can get a hefty dose of help from the good HR people out there. Be careful what you wish for—good HR people also have the courage to challenge leaders no matter how senior their title. Good HR people go to work every day prepared to be fired because often they need to confront leaders about actions and push back on decisions. Good HR people aggressively pursue line leaders who authentically believe in people and want a true partnership that ignites the potential and passions of people because they know once this flame is lit, greatness is kindled.

So that's about all I have to say on this topic—well, maybe one more comment: If leaders keep whining about people and complaining about the complexity of HR, the next headline you may see is: "Why We Hate Managers Who Don't Manage." When I see the headline "Why We Love Managers Who Love People" then I'll know "talent" isn't an orphan anymore.

Evelyn Taylor

Evelyn is the global organization and development manager for Reed Elsevier. In this capacity, she directs leadership development programs and implements several organizational effectiveness efforts across the company. She has successfully implemented an Executive Education program in partnership with Harvard Business School and is currently partnering with Todd Jick and the Global Leadership Services team to design and implement a development process to strengthen and develop General Managers.

Evelyn has been affiliated with InterClass since 2002 as a colleague, friend, and true fan. In her relationship with InterClass she has collaborated on writing, consulting, and "think tank" efforts.

A graduate of GE's prestigious Human Resources Leadership program, Evelyn holds a B.A. from Southern Connecticut State University and a M.A. in counseling/education from Central Connecticut State University. An avid exercise and fitness enthusiast, Evelyn has completed five triathlons.

~~NETWORKS~~
An Emerging Organizational Form for
Creative Collaboration

By Janet Brown & David Swain
Principals, JD Brownfields

Introduction

As the complexity of social problems increases, the need for collaboration—and for effective leadership of collaborative efforts—becomes more apparent. The resolution of contemporary social issues such as urban renewal and economic development, escalating health care costs, occupational health and safety, and homelessness requires commitment and cooperation between two or more organizations. Things may be complicated further still when the organizations that must cooperate exist across the traditional domains of the private and public sectors.

Today's service organizations face ambiguous and complex responsibilities in a time when resources are scarce, problems are complex in depth and scope, and task boundaries are increasingly unclear. An early approach was to link programs across organizations and sectors through the creation of pathways. While this approach made visible the complex connections between organizations addressing common or complementary problems, pathways did not deal with the relationships between the organizations.

Now, the momentum has moved to the organizing level, and new forms of relationships—networks—are being created across organizations through the use of collaborative structures. These new relationships create a context for sharing information and resources, developing and disseminating knowledge, and collective decision making and action taking. The intent of this chapter is to support the growing understanding of these networks, and of the development challenges that they present to leaders.

Features of Networks

Networks are composed of multiple organizations that work collaboratively together to achieve goals that they could not otherwise accomplish. Often the issues are too complex or multi-faceted for an organization to master alone. To support the collaboration, structures and processes are created to enable the network's development, while allowing members to maintain separate identities and potentially disparate goals.

Unique features of networked systems are

- They are multi-organizational in their composition.
- They are under-organized in their structure and consist of fluid membership and loosely coupled relationships.
- Their boundaries are indefinite and highly permeable.

A network system's under-organized structure and mix of loosely coupled relationships, result in an unusual disbursement of power and leadership—one that differs significantly from traditional hierarchically driven or defined systems. In addition, membership and levels of commitment are variable and tend to move and shift over time. These shifts depend on the stage of the network's development and on the nature of the task to be accomplished.

The complexity of these multi-organizational systems creates significant development challenges. If member organizations are to participate as autonomous entities with intact individual identities, potentially disparate goals, and independent decision-making authority and processes, a significant shift is required. The shift is from a traditional organizational egocentric view of problem solving to a collaborative approach with a network-centric perspective. A powerful need or purpose must be developed to sustain this network-centric perspective thus allowing joint decision making and action taking.

Network Context

How to begin, when and how to intervene, and who and how to lead are all significant network development questions. The contexts in which these network systems exist, as well as the needs that create them, are complex. They present significant challenges to the understanding of a planned effort, and of the relevant development issues. When identifying the factors that influence development, three contextual levels must be considered: the general environment, the organization, and the group.

General Environment

The general environment refers to the broad system within which a network is operating. Factors at this level create the imperatives that can demonstrate whether the traditional approaches to problem solving, resource allocation, or governance are effective. Without this imperative, risk-taking and creativity won't emerge within what tends to be a highly competitive, unstable environmental context. Large systems change processes are at the mercy of temperamental fluctuations in the environment, and subsequently large systems find it difficult to cope in times of uncertainty.

Environmental factors influencing network development can be divided into two broad categories: the characteristics of the problem and the characteristics of the organizations involved.

Problem Characteristics	Organizational Characteristics
• Degree of severity and complexity • Nature of the resources available	• Degree of stability • Degree of flexibility • Degree of existing conflict between member organizations

There are two opposing views on what makes an organization a suitable network candidate. One opinion is that a stable system with strong organizational boundaries and relationships, flexible mechanisms for interacting, and low levels of conflict will be better able to support the creation and sustainability of a networked effort. A differing opinion recognizes that networks are most likely to emerge during periods of instability, resource scarcity, and conflict about goals and resource allocation. Therefore, instability, coupled with tasks that are unstructured and highly interdependent, best creates the momentum and readiness necessary to take on a networked approach. While both of these views have merit, the realities of organizational situations are very rarely this clear. Some elements of both views are at work in most organizations. Highly complex problems with limited resource availability provide environmental conditions ripe for creating and sustaining a network.

Organization

The organization context is the network itself. The factors that influence the development and sustained performance are:

- **Interdependence**
  When solving complex social issues, the perceived level of interdependence directly impacts the network's ability to make decisions and take action. Where the players can spot the opportunities and believe in the potential impact of the collaborative effort, they can fundamentally affect the system's ability to simultaneously manage the tension between maintaining organizational autonomy and joining the effort.

- **Organizational Interests**
  The network's ability to work in lateral relationships is directly dependent upon the clear understanding of fundamental organizational interest. Organizational interests are likely related to issues of efficiency, stability, and legitimacy. Sustaining the motivation and commitment of the participants over time can be difficult.

- **Commitment**
  Top-level commitment from the participating organizations must be present in concrete forms, such as resource

allocation and other types of direct sponsorship. The issue of top management commitment relates to the perceived legitimacy of stakeholders, as well as to the power and authority of the convener of the network. These issues are particularly relevant during the initiation stage of the network's development. Over time, power should be redistributed among the stakeholders; otherwise, when a small group of people defines reality for the rest of the network, that small group typically perceives any change in the network as a threat to their power and influence. This significantly limits a network's potential to make positive change. A large system, based on differing value systems and priorities, allows for a much broader spectrum of perspectives and sources of power. In a network, power and politics are diffused and free to shift with time. In essence, traditional, hierarchically defined bases of power do not exist in effective networks.

Areas of Focus	Issue
• Interdependence • Organizational Interests • Top-level Commitment	• Tension between the long-term opportunity for the network and the short-term demands of the member organizations

Group

Considerations within the group context include group interaction and development, power and politics, leadership, and interpersonal relations. Group process issues are further complicated in networks. This is a result of the fluid, loosely bound, highly political nature of these entities. The issues relate primarily to boundaries, culture, and norms. Given the loosely bound relationships and the fluidity of membership in the network, challenges to group development process are significant. Pressure on the network to safeguard the participating members' organizational boundaries further complicates the issue. At the group level, the development focus is on membership, subgroup conflict, and the degree of subgroup identity. In order for collaboration to occur at the subgroup, subgroup identity needs to be low. A strong sense of shared vision and goals must also exist. Of additional significance are interpersonal issues related to trust, communications, and conflict.

Areas of Focus	Issues
• Boundaries • Culture • Norms	• Dealing with the loosely bound, highly political nature of the network's member organizations

Network Development

Network systems move through four predictable stages of development: initiation, exploration, mobilization, and evaluation.

Initiation

In the initiation stage, people and organizations begin to focus on and discuss common problems. Trust, communication, and a mutual understanding are all created as the people involved cluster together and interact on common issues. Through a growing awareness of their interrelatedness on common issues, a compelling reason for continuing and ultimately collaborating evolves.

Potential members of the network are identified, and criteria for participation are established. These criteria are determined based on members' skills, knowledge, and available resources. This is a difficult time for the group; required tasks are often ambiguous, leadership unclear or intermittent, and there is always the potential for lack of cohesion among the participants. Frequently an outside consultant is engaged to help the network gain clarity of purpose, strategic intent, and operating principles.

Primary Focus	Challenges
• Overarching reason for creating the network • Membership composition required to create and sustain results	• Competing sources of influence and legitimacy • Fluid state of membership and participation • Developing a collaborative approach to decision making

Exploration

During exploration, network members must decide whether operating within a collaborative group or network is desirable and feasible. Members spend a great deal of energy on getting people motivated at this point, and the network population attempts to agree on the nature of the tasks. This is a direction-setting stage that includes the identification of group goals and the approaches and actions required to achieve the goals.

Members typically begin to recognize that a collaborative approach is both possible and likely to be productive. Momentum builds toward collective action and mobilization. In addition, as the group identifies common values and purposes, a sense of group cohesion begins to form. At this stage a consultant often supports network communications and conflict resolution, and—in the absence of a designated leader—serves as an activist within the system.

Primary Focus	Challenges
• Establishing a commitment to problem solving • Establishing a mandate for the network	• Members struggle to abide by collaborative decisions in the face of organizational demands • Maintaining member focus and involvement

Mobilization

In mobilization, the group's focus shifts from mandate and task identification to the establishment of structures and mechanisms for accomplishing goals. The group's activities become more formal as rules, policies, and operating procedures are established. Costs and benefits are further refined, including considerations of the members' legal obligations and contractual rights.

As the group members work to establish a common compatible purpose, it is important that the leader focus on structure, leadership, communications processes, and ways to positively assess progress. These issues, along with the development of integrating mechanisms, may prove critical for sustaining the network effort.

It is common during this stage for a powerful leader to emerge, or for a coordinating leadership council to be formed and for the role of the consultant to begin to diminish.

Primary Focus	Challenges
• Formalization of structures and mechanisms to accomplish work • Formalizing new roles, responsibilities and expectations	• Delivering on promised commitments and resources • Developing sustainable network leadership and governance

Evaluation

At this stage, members are focused on evaluation. The effectiveness of the network's collaborative decision making and action taking is measured. A network's ultimate goal is simple: to act together to undertake tasks that could not be accomplished alone. The measurement of how effective a network is in reaching that goal, however, can be complex. It is also difficult to evaluate the satisfaction of its members.

The evaluation can be approached from a number of perspectives, including

• Community-level or broader system-level impact. This can

be considered in terms of the impact and quality of problem solving, general shifts in attitudes, and general shifts in
decision-making processes.

- Functional effectiveness of the network. The measure of the
functional effectiveness of the network itself is specifically
related to its ability to accomplish its mandate and goals.
Ultimately, a network's sustainability and ability to expand
its collaborative agenda will be the prime measure of its
effectiveness.

- Individual/Group-level performance and satisfaction indicators. At the group level, outcomes are personal levels of
satisfaction and motivation, effectiveness of group's process,
and increased personal effectiveness.

Primary Focus	Challenges
• Evaluating performance • Assessing satisfaction	• Agreement on evaluation criteria • Use of evaluation data to further development and sustain the performance of the network

All of the measures of progress must be considered within the context of the stage of group development and growth.

Leadership Support

In the context of a network, the concept of the leader is much
more fluid than in most traditional organizations. It can be a single role
that shifts between members depending on the situations faced by the network, and, at times, it can also be the role of a small group. In developing
and sustaining networks, leaders must play a non-traditional role. Leaders of traditional, hierarchical organizations have power and control that
comes from their position in the organization's structure. They can command resources and have control over the extrinsic motivational factors
used to direct and reward performance. In a network, this command and

control does not exist at the same level. Networks require a different set of leadership behaviors; the leader must focus on managing two dimensions: energy and structure. Energy and structure are critical to the development and sustainability of the network. Due to the unique nature of networks, leaders often find it useful to engage a consultant to support them and the network during the first three stages of development.

Energy

During the early stages of development, energy in the network must be maintained at a high level. Energy is the excitement, engagement, interest, and passion displayed by the network members. The leader helps maintain this energy by supporting the creation and enrollment of members in a shared vision—what they can only accomplish together. The leader is also on the lookout to identify and enroll additional potential members that would add to the network's ability to accomplish its goals. New members need to be connected directly into the network, and not just through the leader. The leader must be willing to relinquish traditional desires for control, and instead trust in the network's shared purpose: to do the right things. At these early stages, the leader's role is facilitation, synthesis and sense making, connection making, and encouragement.

As the network moves into the latter half of exploration, the network should begin to be self-energizing. At this point the leader needs to add a focus on sustainable structures within the network, and aid in their development. Before focusing on structure, however, the network needs a robust, energizing, and motivating sense of shared purpose. If a network's focus on structure happens too early, the leader should resist these efforts. Supporting a premature adoption of structure will dissipate the energy required to fully explore the shared purpose, and may ultimately negatively affect the network's potential for sustenance.

Structure

At this point, the shared purpose is developed, and members are engaged and excited. When the leader senses that the network is becoming self-energizing, then some of their focus must shift to the development of structure. Structuring is the development of integrating mechanisms to support the ongoing functioning of the network. The leader's role is to help broker the necessary agreements that the member organizations, as part of their participation, may require. Networks are different from traditional organizations in that the structure they require is less rigid and more permeable. The network consistently adapts to changes in its environment and membership, and so develops a structure that recognizes these realities. The establishment of network internal leadership is critical to the functioning of the network. Will the network be led by a single individual, or by a team of individuals? The relationships and politics of the member organizations within the network will be constantly evolving, and the leader must be aware of this. This understanding provides the leader with the insight necessary to guide an internal leadership approach that will maintain the energy of the network, and ultimately its sustainability.

The leader's primary role, throughout the life of the network, is to continually kindle the network's shared purpose. This is accomplished through consistent reminders. A leader reminds the members of their network's intent through their actions, focus, and storytelling. Story telling is one of the best approaches to explaining the network's reason for being, and for conveying the progress being made.

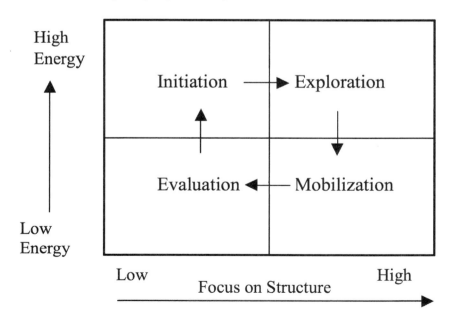

Summary

Leaders play a different role in the development of these types of organizations than they do in traditional hierarchical organizations. Networks are held together and driven by their shared purpose, not by the power and control used to manage traditional organizations. Current organizational structures do not adequately address the tensions of competition/collaboration and change/stability. The very factors and motivations that create readiness for implementing these new approaches make it difficult to sustain their ability to act collaboratively. Acknowledging these tensions and supporting their co-existence may be a necessary requirement for moving from a traditional, hierarchical perspective to a more network-based model.

Network systems operating in the public sector can be large, complex, and unwieldy entities. A leader can quickly become immersed in the complexity of the structure and its supporting mechanisms. They must attend to the needs of the individuals involved, understand their motivations, and support them in acquiring the skills, linkages, and resources needed to sustain the network. The stages of group development are as relevant to the success of networks as with groups within traditional organizations. Leaders must understand that the complicating impact of shifting membership to the group development process is central to working with the individuals involved.

Sustainability factors that are critical to network systems include the creation of reliable linkages to support information sharing, knowledge development/dissemination, communications, and ways to positively assess progress. Networks exist in parallel to member organizations and other entities in the community. Moving the network into a more integrating role, through the creation of linkages and mechanisms, is critical to its effectiveness and sustainability. Finally, strategic intent and purpose must be continually focused and refined. In assessing how best to first define strategic intent and purpose, leaders need to consider the complex interaction between leaders, sponsors, and external change agents. At the same time, the effective leader is always aware of the network's evolving nature.

The development of networks as an emerging organizational form offers new opportunities to deal with what appear to be unsolvable problems. Networks naturally emerge; a phenomenon that reflects the complex nature of the problems and pressures currently confronting public and private sector organizations. Current thinking about how organizations relate to each other and how work gets done requires a fundamental realignment—this is how organizations will find solutions to the challenges currently facing them. Networks provide a window to furthering our understanding.

David Swain

David Swain is a management consultant and co-principal of JDBrownfields, a consulting firm based in Toronto, Canada. His career began in sales where he held leadership positions with Pacific Bell, Advance Information Systems, and AT&T. David then co-founded LEAGACY Alliance, a consulting business founded on the body of leadership work developed by Dr. Warren Bennis (USC). David's experience also includes acting as learning team leader for the Emerging Leader and Executive Team Programs at the Global Institute for Leadership, and consulting experience with a range of private, public, and not-for-profit sector organizations in North America and Europe. More recently, David completed a five-year term as national managing partner of Integrated Services, Deloitte USA, where David also contributed as the co-developer and lead faculty for the U.S. Leadership Forum (Leadership 2000) for Deloitte & Touche's top 180 partners. Throughout his career, David has been focused on the role effective leadership plays in the performance of organizations through times of crisis, opportunity, and growth. He holds a BS in Management and an MS in organization development and strategic change.

David has been a member of InterClass since 1993 and involved in InterClass consulting engagements since 2006.

Janet Brown

Janet Brown, MBA, MSOD has been providing management consulting support in the private, not-for-profit and public sectors for over 20 years. Her passion lies in the health care sector, and the challenges presented to health care leaders by the complexity of the operating environment, the constant need for change, and the pressure to continually balance the diverse needs and interests of the many stakeholders and partners. Janet has worked with organizations such as the Ontario Workplace Safety & Insurance Board, Levi Strauss Canada, the Ontario Ministry of Health, and several Ontario based hospitals including Women's College Hospital, Hamilton Health Sciences, Sick Children's Hospital, and St. Michael's Hospital. Most recently, Janet has been involved in the establishment of a Research Centre in Occupational Disease—a partnership between St. Michael's Hospital and the University of Toronto. Janet is also currently supporting the development of the Learning Institute at Sick Children's Hospital. Janet is co-principal of JDBrownfields, a consulting firm based in Toronto, Ontario.

WHAT'S GROWING OURSELVES GOT TO DO WITH GROWING OUR BUSINESS?

By Zeynep Tozum

Farbeyond Consulting

During the past six years that I've rejoiced working in the field of performance development, I've become more and more intrigued by the fact that the link between business growth and personal growth can so easily fall outside the repertoire of most leaders. In this chapter, I will talk about some observations and insights that help me understand this phenomenon as well as some thoughts on how I see performance coaching making an impact on executives who are willing to explore this link.

According to a survey by the Conference Board, an American business research association, "sustained and steady growth" is at the top of the list of America's CEOs concerns. Business growth is seen as the ultimate success parameter, more than ever before, shifting the attention of executives from saving costs and improving margins to creating new markets, products, and customers. Consequently, companies with a sustainable track record in growth and the ideas and executions that got them there are the key features of many articles and interviews. However, while most of the "magic" is attributed to new insights, breakthrough ideas, clever executions, and change projects, it is almost unheard of that a CEO talks about the personal development (growth) he/she went through while trying to find their swing in leading the business to growth.

Tom Peters says, "To make a mark on the outside, a company needs soul, spirit, character and personality on the inside." A company is its employees and if growth is the mark then there needs to be a direct link between the growth of a business and that of its leaders and managers.

When we think a business is stuck, it usually means that we hold, in our minds, a picture of what's possible in its current market or industry and we are bound by the limitations of that picture. In fact, being able to break through these limitations is what leads to new business creation and growth. No business is ever the same if it sustains its new territory long enough to actually bump into totally new limitations. How amazingly similar to what an individual experiences on his/her path to growth!

The Disconnect At Play

Just think of a business that produces extraordinary results, resets industry success metrics through its rapid growth, a business that marries solid strategy and systems with a way of doing business where both individuals and teams operate at their best, where there is a strong sense of purpose that drives people beyond the comfort of a pay-check, where business growth is an opportunity, a way to actualize individual dreams.

Is this an excerpt from a corporate story book, or could it be real? For many of us, it is a remote possibility or even worse, a naïve vision. What would sound more real is that we often witness our business getting stuck in declining markets, enslaved to sharply rising costs and to altered customer behaviors. As we reluctantly agree to the next year's business plan, committing to a growth target that we can't even conceive wipes away any possible excitement or confidence we might have developed so far. Knowing no savvy leader would dare to question the need to grow the business, we go ahead and plunge into the soothing comfort of being in action: running innovation workshops, setting up project teams, building plans. Our staff meeting speeches emphasize how much drive, commitment, and resilience is needed to deliver on the plans—and that we need to act with courage in order to reach our growth targets. There is a wave of energy in the room and people leave with a sense of liberation ("I am not the only one thinking it is going to be tough") and some kind of curious hopefulness ("everything's going to change and we will make it"). After all, we just had our restructuring, revised our business strategy, and designed a new organizational structure. So we should get there, right? Maybe.

I want to assert that, beyond these obvious—and required—steps, growth of a business requires an attitude adjustment. Those who are the key players in the leadership game need to reinvent themselves while rethinking the business.

In fact, the "new age wisdom" of the business world already focuses, more than ever, on growing leadership. And yet, acknowledgement of the causality between business growth and personal growth seems to be restricted to training rooms, leadership conferences, and intellectual debates. I am often intrigued by the disconnect between these two concepts, especially at times when the business is under severe pressure to perform. I remember a company chairman actually saying this to me, "We will definitely look into our leadership capacities and how we work together but right now, my first priority is to hit my annual plan. Then, we can take some time and look into what we need as an organization." Another indication of the disconnect is the reluctance of top executives to work with a performance coach, to admit it when they do, and to share their personal growth goals or the experience and transformation they went through.

Personal Growth: A Soft Concept Serving the Hard End of Performance

Most of us believe that our analytical capacity, sharpness, and logic are our primary assets and that if we are good enough, they will clear our heads as well as our way to the top. And yes, clarity and speed of thinking gets us noticed, and helps us fly high. Yet, as long as we are unaware of what emotional—and mostly automatic—responses drive our choices, we can't break through them when they don't work for us. We end up with dry logic and acid leadership—and we get stuck in the ranks.

Any successful business achievement could in fact be tracked down to a moment in time, when a team or a person has made a choice or taken an action. Apart from professional skills, that person or team's beliefs, attitude, and world view have an undeniable impact on the quality of that choice or decision. This is not to deny the power of our intellect but to assert that to use it effectively, we need to be at our best. (By best, I mean emotionally cleverest.) Getting to that wisdom requires first an awareness of what is so, what pushes our buttons, what unproductive responses, limitations, and competing intentions we have. We then can look at our ambitions, restate what we want, and chose what behavioral shifts we want to achieve to get there. The resulting work can alter the substance of how we lead, beyond a mere change in form. This is how a soft concept like personal growth can stand right at the hard end of performance.

The Gift of Discomfort

When the execution of big ideas is slow and clumsy, when board meetings are mostly spent on status reviews, when issues persist despite many projects, when the impact of the "team building day" or the "off-site meeting" fades out in weeks, there is clearly a performance issue. And yet, I have often observed in my first contact with top executives that they see the performance of their team/organization somewhat (or in some cases totally) independent from their own capabilities—if only their team members would be more responsible, more committed, more visionary. Change is often mentioned in these talks as something that their people have to go through.

What are these smart and able leaders not wanting to see, and why not? What's missing as an approach? The answer I suggest lies in the discomfort we human beings feel as soon as we start suspecting we might not be perfect and that we will be dangerously dangling on the edge of our limitations if we ever want to go for a significant challenge.

The resulting resistance keeps most leaders away from grabbing opportunities for self-development; instead, they choose blaming the market conditions and the lack of skills in their people for the stagnating business results. Paradoxically, this experience of discomfort when confronted with self-challenge could in fact be the spark of awareness, pointing to the hidden need or growth edge, which, if seized as an opportunity (rather than a problem), could prove to be a gift.

Supporting Growth through Performance Coaching

We can all think of moments when we witnessed a breakthrough idea hitting our Board Room or a totally new opportunity emerging almost from nowhere in a project meeting. What was different? Where did the sharpness come from? How did we start seeing a business target as a challenging opportunity and no more an obligation? How come we stopped wanting to be right and started supporting someone else's clever idea instead? Where did the stress go? How could we already see how we could grow our turnover in a year's time to an unprecedented rate? How did we get to our best? Could we recreate that day?

Being there is not magic but possibly the result of some collective and individual work leading to that level of alignment, purposeful action, and creativity. To get on that path, the challenge is to get curious enough to discover more about ourselves and humble enough to accept support. Among many forms of professional, organized support, I believe coaching is the most practical road to growing the business. Coaching can significantly accelerate the process for individuals and teams to see new possibilities, articulate an ambition, choose what they want to work on to get there, and use the business context to frame this work.

Building Clarity of What Is So

To set out on the road to personal development, all we need to know is what we really want, why we want that, and what blocks us. This is where it gets tricky: we are blind to many of our qualities, as well as to our dysfunctional behaviors and limiting beliefs. Being smart is not enough unless we have surrounded ourselves with support. Many of the leaders I have worked with would talk enthusiastically about what's missing in their team and how they want them to behave differently but would rarely mention a word about their own limitations. Likewise, they would not necessarily know their own unique strengths that could be relied on at times of trouble or discomfort.

Getting to know ourselves is not that difficult. As we can't really see ourselves, we just need others' eyes to do that for us. However, not many of us are comfortable with asking for feedback, nor are we trained to welcome and process what we hear. For most leaders, asking for feedback is a rare act of courage unless they are sure they will like what they will hear. On the other hand, giving feedback is often used as a way of dumping our judgments onto others and rarely seen as a gift we give to someone we care about. Consequently, people often fall in the trap of wanting to please or look good and thus avoid telling the truth about what they are seeing. The coach, however, through confidential and trusting conversations, can gather data about the person from this outside world, from subordinates, fellow team members, and bosses. The coach would also help the person grasp insights, patterns, and beliefs and frame the issue and therefore the opportunity, in light of what's possible.

Choosing and Committing to a Purpose

The next challenge is whether we really want to stretch ourselves and hold the discomfort of playing in an unfamiliar field. That field can sometimes be as simple as learning to listen when we have mostly been talking in an urge to inspire, or accepting that there may be more than one way of doing it right when we tend to convince others that our way is best. What will ease that discomfort is the notion of purpose. Personal growth may be too abstract to keep the person focused. The coach could help the person articulate a challenge and find an exciting purpose to aim for, one that will make a big difference to his/her business results. The mere fact that a coach is hired already says that the challenge involved is pretty big. To match that challenge, there needs to be a strong commitment from the player that will help her/him stay in the game when times get tough. The coach will look for that commitment that will anchor the leader.

Learning through Practice

Growing the self, by learning to act with purpose, commitment, responsibility, and courage can be as difficult as growing a business in a stagnant economy and yet, it sounds less concrete, soft, and therefore less important. Words around personal growth and leadership are spoken so very often as part of inspirational speeches, leadership development programs, and team building events that they lose their ability to evoke curiosity in our minds. What we miss is a true experience of these abstract concepts to give us a concrete picture of how they could serve us in creating and growing businesses.

There are many ways to get to try new ways that will help us achieve more, and coaching is only one of them. However, when sustained performance and learning is the objective then coaching can be much more effective than being advised or mentored as it will help with intensifying practices and turning them into habits. The coach helps the person dare to look at what works and what does not, to see more options and to practice, thus stretching her/his abilities beyond current limitations. The feedback loop becomes the compass and guides the journey. Despite your commitment, if the rest of your Board of Directors was not enrolled into your business idea, the coaching session will take you beyond blaming others or your self-accusations and help you nail down what drove that outcome and what was missing. New ways of dealing with similar situations will emerge from that blend of encouragement and challenge the coach brings.

Gaining Affinity for Growth

Soon, new patterns of thinking become new habits of the leader's mind that later on will, with or without a coach in the process, open up the leader's perspective on getting things done through others and creating collectively. Furthermore, when we experiment and innovate new ways of being, when our team/business responds rapidly, when we can see changes in our business results, we often discover a new pleasure fueled by feeling awake, purposeful, and powerful through personal discovery and growth. That often leads to an affinity for further growth. We are launched on a new path.

On the other hand, I have at times seen that this experience coupled with the wonderful comfort of finding a safe, trusted, intelligent, and caring ally in the coach can drive executives to a latent dependency towards their coach. It is therefore crucial to make sure that the coach leaves the leader with skills and ability to deepen awareness, to ask powerful questions, to look for feedback and support when in need, and to sustain personal growth without the continuous help of a coach. This is the ultimate test for real learning and growth.

A Last Word

It can be amazingly refreshing and productive for a leader to have a brand new and courageous perspective on what it takes to move a business to growth—considering yourself as a project in service of the growth you want to create in your business. It will be a process of discovering, choosing and learning, taking you on a ride, transforming the way you lead, and potentially touching your other relationships: with your kids, your partner, and your friends!

Your capacity to produce is increased! That is personal growth; that is being at your best, at the hard end of business performance.

Zeynep Tozum

Zeynep Tozum is an organizational development consultant and an executive performance coach who works with businesses, executives, and teams around the world. She spent 20 years working for Unilever, primarily in marketing, business restructuring, cost management, and change. She then joined Unilever corporate as vice president, performance development, and supporting transformation in operating companies around the world. Along the way, executive coaching became an integral part of her consulting work. She later set up her own practice, FARBEYOND CONSULTING in organizational development. She calls herself a genuine Turk and a world citizen, with cultural diversity nurtured by her country as well as by her education and work over a diverse geography. She sees her work as her way of impacting the world: through her and others' growth, she encourages businesses and leaders to stretch and bring out their best. In order to "lead" our lives, she believes in reinventing ourselves with purpose, clarity, and resilience; hence her interest in leadership and its results. She met Eric and Robin through her work and says she found true partners and mentors in them, stimulating her thinking and creativity.

PART II
The InterClass Process

Edited by Eric E. Vogt and Robin Grumman-Vogt

Part II Overview
The InterClass Process

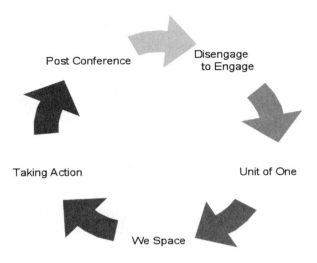

The InterClass Process—the processes and methods we use at InterClass sessions—mirrors interactive methods used by leaders who know how to consistently engage their organizations in productive conversations. Productive conversations enable organizations to reach their full potential. Productive conversations focus on the questions pivotal to an organization's success in both business and human terms. In short, there is a continuous cycle of—

- inquiry
- exploration
- action and
- support of individuals and groups

that empowers this kind of conversational engagement.

Leaders who successfully engage in these kinds of conversations support cultures that enable and explicitly understand that their human talent needs to be able to have ways of recognizing that each associate is a whole person with many facets to their lives. This enables disengagement from concerns and opportunities in non-work domains so that each associate can more fully engage in the work of their organizations. We call this process "Disengage to Engage" and it is discussed in Chapter 1.

It can be difficult for associates to participate in group processes especially decision-making processes if they have not had an opportunity (time and information) to develop an individual perspective. In Chapter 2 on the "Unit of One" we talk about processes that enable associates to be fully present in their work conversation because they have had a chance to develop insight and a loosely held point of view.

There are many ways to effectively engage the many in a conversation of importance. In Chapter 3 on "The We Space" we talk about how InterClass accomplishes this in sessions and how leaders can support the same kind of dynamic in their organizations.

Even when an organization is ready to take action the conversation needs to continue to ensure coordination through consensus building and preparation. We discuss this in Chapter 4 on "Taking Action."

The work is never over in terms of what can be learned. Conversations enable ongoing support of the community involved and the harvesting of valuable individual and group reflections that enable future improvements. This is true both while a body of work or a conference are underway and after they are complete. This perspective is covered in Chapter 5 on "Post Conference."

The next five chapters discuss the processes and methods we use in InterClass sessions and extrapolate from these methods similar processes that are needed by effective leaders in the 21st century. The purpose of each of the processes we use in an InterClass session is summarized in the table that follows.

InterClass Session Process

Process Component	Purpose
1. **Disengage to Engage**	• Getting to know participants and their organizations' issues and opportunities • Becoming free to participate • Being present in the moment
2. **Unit of One**	• Grounding in what I feel, in who I am • Grounding in what I think
3. **We Space**	• Developing perspectives • Sharing and refining perspectives • Surfacing assumptions and mental models • Absorbing and practicing content through games and simulations
4. **Action**	• Reaching consensus on actions to take • Preparing to take action
5. **Post Conference**	• Supporting community • Harvesting reflections

Whether you are reading the next five chapters with the eye of a facilitator of interactive sessions or an interactive leader of organizations we hope that our writings will be of service.

CHAPTER ONE

DISENGAGE TO ENGAGE

In order to engage deeply with a complex problem, we need to free ourselves of old patterns of conditioned responses and defensive actions that constrain our ability to innovate.

What this chapter is about...

We often hear that an InterClass event feels like an oasis—a place where people are able to temporarily put aside the concerns and constraints that they experience in their everyday work lives, and renew their energy and clarity of purpose. By participating in ways not common to their everyday practices, members return to their work environment refreshed and reinvigorated. The paradox here is that by setting aside the pressing concerns of daily work, InterClass participants often find they return to work with new ideas and solutions to what may have seemed intractable problems.

Why these techniques work...

Cognitive scientists have long known that in order to learn something, we often have to unlearn something else. This is particularly true for adult learners, who come fully equipped with a lifetime of experiences, associations, and assumptions, not all of them positive. When facing a new challenge, conventional ways of thinking can constrain our ability to discover a creative new approach. Thus, in order to engage deeply with a complex problem, we need to free ourselves of old patterns of conditioned responses and defensive actions that constrain our ability to innovate. Thus, to move forward, we sometimes need to stop what we're doing. To engage more deeply, we need first to disengage from the daily grind that threatens to keep us from ever making the breakthroughs that our organizations—and we as humans—need in order to achieve success.

Why these techniques matter to leaders...

This chapter will explore some of the particular techniques at InterClass we use to achieve this effect. Leaders can use these techniques to help their people disengage to engage—a critical technique for getting the best from a workforce. By following the flow of an InterClass event, we will introduce our essential norms and core techniques. Then we'll show how these concepts and tools can be applied to help leaders master the day-to-day challenges they face in managing their organizations.

InterClass Norms

An essential feature of InterClass meetings is ensuring that all participants feel free to fully participate, that they feel that they are in a trusting environment. At the beginning of each meeting, we set the tone by sharing the InterClass norms. Norms are ways of doing things based on deep-seated beliefs and core values. Every organization has them, but they are not always made explicit.

Norms are ways of doing things based on deep-seated beliefs and core values. Every organization has them, but they are not always made explicit.

Here at InterClass we believe that it's essential to our success that every participant understand, embrace, and practice these norms. Because they're so important to us, we take time at the beginning of every meeting to review and talk them over with participants.

Even long-time members say how much they value this reminder of what matters to the network, and how helpful this conversation is in setting the tone for what's to come.

Let's look at each of these norms in turn:

1. High trust
2. Diversity
3. Consensus
4. Confidentiality
5. Hard on ideas, soft on people
6. Learn from each other/Learn from failure
7. Experiment with new approaches
8. Consultancies: Truthful and thoughtful feedback

Norm #1: High Trust

High trust is the first norm needed to create an oasis. Because it serves as the foundation for all our other norms, it's the one we focus on most.

Trusting through Explication

It's helpful to actively define what we mean by trust. We use the word *trust* when we share assessments about people and interactions, assuming there is a common understanding about what it means. But there is often disagreement and tension around trust because of the absence of an explicit shared definition. By defining trust and bringing an emotionally charged word out into the open, we create a sense of ease so that our interactions can be observed, described, and acted upon. By talking about something that usually goes unsaid, we reduce emotional overhead and enable trust to be an essential component for business and personal interactions.

This is the first example of a pattern we'll see throughout InterClass—of surfacing what is often buried, of making explicit the tacit, in order to release those assumptions and biases that can hold us back, and keep us from seeing things with fresh eyes.

At InterClass we define trust as the ability to depend. Trust involves four types of dependability. When I say I trust someone completely that means I trust them on all four of the following dimensions:

- They are **sincere** in what they say, their words are consistent at different times and with different listeners; they intend to do what they commit to
- They have the **competence** to fulfill their commitments
- They are **reliable**; they have a pattern of doing what they say they will
- They demonstrate commitment to the **relationship** through ongoing interactions during and between commitments

At InterClass when someone expresses concern about trusting an individual or entity we go through an exercise to discover whether their assessment involves sincerity, reliability, competence, or relationship. The resulting answers often reduce the emotional charge and add a clarity that becomes actionable, allowing for the delineation of the circumstances under which a particular person or organization can or cannot be trusted. By talking through these issues, those affected often find they are able to reset their relationship and mend or prevent a rift.

Checking In

To free participants to fully participate, we often provide an opportunity to put away concerns they may carry with them when they come to an InterClass event. The process we use is called *checking-in*. It's amazingly simple and amazingly powerful. We go around the room and give participants two minutes apiece to describe, i.e., check-in, any concerns or pre-occupations that could get in the way of their being fully present during the meeting. The idea here is something like parking a car. Participants park their car in the garage—and in this case, their nagging issues—and they can then go forward onto new activities, knowing their concerns are protected and will be there when they're ready to pick them up and go home.

This technique is doable inside corporate environments as well. It was used extensively by the organization development function at a global apparel company in the 1990s. Their facilitators promoted nothing happening, not even an agenda review, before a check-in was done with everyone in the room. It helps people concentrate on the task at hand and be fully present in the moment. When leaders support this kind of practice it also shows that they recognize their co-workers as full human beings with needs and concerns outside of the workplace as well as within. It is another method of demonstrating work-family balance, especially when the leader acknowledges concerns or interests of their own outside daily work life.

Trusting through Membership

InterClass is explicit in asking participants to operate from an assumption of trust. Our definition of trust pervades everything we do, from the way we run events to the way we choose our members. From their very first days in the network, InterClass members know they are there because of the trust

No competing organizations as members at the same time.

extended to them by other members. It is a long-standing InterClass policy to have no competing organizations as members at the same time. Competing status is determined by our members. If a new proposed member is seen as a competitor by an existing member then that organization will not receive an invitation to join the InterClass network. Likewise, any new participant has received a personal invitation from InterClass members or staff who already have a trusting relationship with that individual. We ask, too, that these first-time participants extend that sense of trust to the entire InterClass network.

Trust can be directly experienced or it can be conferred. At first, a new participant operates under conferred trust, which works like this: "I was invited here by Cary, whom I trust. I know Cary trusts everyone in the InterClass network, therefore I will trust them, too." At the same time that we promote this assumption of trust, we also recognize that each participant can only operate on their own trustworthiness, that is, "I cannot control others so that they always behave in a trustworthy manner, but I can ensure my behavior and words come from a place of authenticity and trust."

Trusting through Understanding

Another component of establishing trust is having knowledge of the other people in the room. Our staff spends time between our engagements staying in touch with our members through phone calls, email, and via our on-line network to be sure we understand the concerns and aspirations of the organizations that make up InterClass. We also use surveys before and after meetings to gather and refine our understanding of the key topics the InterClass network has defined as important that year. Because we are constantly in touch on common issues, we are continually sharpening our awareness of each others' concerns and opportunities. As a result, we are also building our collective capacity to address each others' needs.

InterClass staff members also gather news items about members and share the news with other members as quickly as possible. This knowledge of our members enables them to feel that we know them and they know each other. It is also a simple way of showing that we care about them and the issues that are important to their organizations. Because InterClass handles introductions and updates on our members, they do not have to spend time or energy explaining themselves or their organization, and so are freer to engage with each other in the present moment. By staying connected with our membership, we enhance our knowledge of each other, and reinforce our mutual trust.

Leading Through Trusting

When leaders find themselves having issues of trust within their organizations, defining the source and sharing a definition and intention around trust can go a long way towards improving levels of trust and freeing employees to more fully participate and engage. Defining trust can enable clear diagnoses of the causes of trust breakdowns. A statement of intention, akin to the InterClass view that all participants must come to our events with an assumption of trust towards everyone else present, enables an organization to explicitly see where it is that the leadership wants to take the organization with regard to the domain of trust. It enables clear language for feedback—"your words are seen as sincere but your actions are not reliable"—both to and from an organization's leaders. This is a simpler intervention to describe than to initiate. It can mean a sea change in an organization's culture. And it needs to be taken on when trust is at the core of an organization's failure to live up to its potential.

> **Case Study from InterClass Consulting: A Story of Trust in Action**
>
> The Latin America division of a global firm was in shambles. Traditionally run as a series of fiefdoms, a recent re-organization had created matrices and organizational inter-dependencies without generating the relationships required to make the new organization work. Regions were warring with each other, and little coordinated thinking or action could take place. Meanwhile, its major competitor was taking market share. A new leader was put in charge of the region, let's call him Val. He toured the region, asked questions, listened, and then called a meeting of the 60 leaders in Rio de Janeiro. When they all arrived at the swank hotel on Copacabana, Val put them on buses and took them to an empty warehouse in a poor Favela. He said, "These people have almost nothing, and their children have little hope in life. We are going to turn this warehouse into a community center for the children over the next 48 hours. Paint and materials are here, and all of the resources of our company are at your disposal. Let's make a difference in their world." In the celebration two days later the parents and children came to the new center, the source of new possibilities in life. They brought churrasco and cashasa (traditional Brazilian foods); the executives brought their hearts. There was not a dry eye in the house. By the end of the evening the warring presidents of the regions were playing the guitar and singing together for the first time. The next morning Val simply said, "If we can work together like this, then we can change the world. From here forward, there will be no further conversations about the organization. They are a waste of time. Let us now take our new found level of trust, and work together to serve our customers like we served this deserving community." Thereafter, Latin America grew at a compound rate of 15% per year.

Using Trust

Leaders of organizations have opportunities to apply many of these same techniques to gain deeper understanding of the people in their organization. Many organizations conduct employee surveys. Surveys can reveal information about what employees believe they

Anonymous surveys **reported back** *to employees build trust.*

need in order to perform at the highest levels possible. Many employees are polled on how they can better serve their customers. All too often, though, the data provided by these tools does not become usable information. Sometimes, the data never gets back to front-line employees; leadership hears about the data but it is not made actionable or relevant to employees.

Leaders of large organizations can't know the concerns and aspirations of each of their employees, but surveys can help them understand the top five concerns of their employees as a collective. More importantly, by referring to this data in their messages to and conversations with employees, leaders can underscore the importance of employee input and highlight the ways that the organization is acting upon the input. By making explicit the feelings and issues that lie under the surface of everyday organizational life, leaders can achieve a new level of authenticity and trustworthiness.

It's one thing for managers to possess a significant understanding of the barriers that prevent higher performance by their teams, but to move from data to action, they must first acknowledge the truth of what the organization is saying by saying it back to the organization. People are enormously empowered when they hear their feelings articulated by a leader. When they hear expressed what is in their hearts and minds, employees are free to move forward in the knowledge that they have been heard.

A leader's ability to converse with genuine interest on the needs and concerns of their people does not mean that a leader needs to have one-on-one conversations with everyone. The conversations of a leader are like the ripples in a pond—they radiate outward far from their point of origin. Because they are so amplified and spread so far within the organization, it's critical that individual conversations are authentic and meaningful. Leaders who monitor the external environment for news about issues of general interest to their employees—such as community and environmental concerns—and use this information in their daily conversations can further demonstrate their commitment to and engagement with employees.

Leaders can't stop there, of course. Action must be taken to address issues, to lower barriers and increase productive ways of meeting organizational goals. But the first step is rooted in bringing forward that which lies within, in authentic speech, in trust. When employee concerns, which are usually rooted in the past, are clearly addressed by leadership, the organization can then focus on future achievement.

Norm #2: Diversity

Diversity has three main components at InterClass: diversity of thinking, diversity of job experience, and diversity of industry.

Diversity of thinking is what enables the innovative ideas and creative strategies of our members to emerge. We believe that diversity of thinking stems from the presence of all other forms of diversity, be it age, gender, race, ethnicity, sexual preference, religion, or experience.

Diversity also encompasses differences in job experiences among our members. Given that the mission of InterClass is to *"explore innovations at the intersection of business strategy and human performance to enable the emergence of leaders and business models, which support high-performing, sustainable organizations,"* it is not surprising that over 50% of our membership in any particular year tends to be made up of heads of human resources, chief learning officers, and leaders of talent management and organization development. In order to achieve the full business view and diverse thinking required by this same purpose, the other 50% of our membership is made up of holders of diverse positions ranging from CIO to heads of marketing, corporate strategy, customer insights, and corporate social responsibility.

Diversity in the InterClass norms also refers to a broad range of industries represented in our membership. Since the founding of InterClass in1990, we have seen innumerable times how ideas from one industry can offer insights to another—most notably between manufacturing and service organizations and between business and the public sector. Diversity is also reflected in our selection of "design teams"—the individuals from our network we assemble to help us design and plan our conferences. We strive to include a number of different points of view in our conference design conversations so that the end result will be of value to a broad spectrum of interests. We have also found great benefit in drawing on our personal networks of forward-thinking leaders and scholars. When thinking through the major business issues of our time, we do not welcome, but actively recruit, the participation of thought partners who can contribute unique perspectives and ideas. Breakthrough thinking can result when rich ideas from one knowledge domain brush up against the best thinking of another.

Norm #3: Consensus

There is never any voting at InterClass. This avoids obvious demarcations of who is on which side of an issue and creates an environment in which conversation continues until there is a clear **consensus**. Consensus is defined at InterClass as 80% comfort, 100% support. This method is most frequently encountered in the InterClass environment when we are deciding on the research agenda for the coming year. The use of consensus frees participants to fully speak their minds without being afraid of being labeled or wedded to a particular perspective. Using consensus also allows participants the freedom to visibly change their minds without being seen as vacillating.

Norm #4: Confidentiality

High trust is also lived through our sense of **confidentiality**. Our norms enable anything to be shared within the room, with the full knowledge that what's said there, stays there, unless specifically invited by the speaker to share it widely.

Norm #5: Hard on Ideas, Soft on People

InterClass has always promoted intellectual passion in its research conferences, but of equal importance has been a keen respect for individuals and their feelings. This has resulted in a norm called "Hard on ideas, soft on people." Much of this has to do with choice of language. At

InterClass you never hear phrases like "I disagree with you." You may well hear "I disagree" or even more likely "that idea is not supported by....." Careful avoidance of even inadvertent criticism of the speaker is promoted. This norm clearly results in more interactions by a greater diversity of participants and a better sense of camaraderie in general, all supportive of the high trust environment that is InterClass.

Norms #6 & 7: Learn from Each Other/Learn from Failure & Experiment with New Approaches

The two penultimate norms—Learn from each other/Learn from failure and Experiment with new approaches—are deeply inter-connected with each other and the learning process we foster at InterClass events. While we do invite thought partners and experts in particular fields to share their knowledge with us during Inter-Class events, we hear from our members that learning from the experience of other organizations represents the true gold mined at InterClass. Because of the trust and commitment our members share, they are able to relate stories of their successes—AND accounts of times when things haven't gone quite so well. We find that our collective experience is far more valuable than the experience of any one of us. By helping each other learn from the failures that we have all been through, we enable each other to see how past failure can become a future success. A manufacturing member had a "file drawer" he called "my failures that were within an inch of being successful." He often brought experience to light that other members used to avoid similar unnecessary mishaps.

Learning from the experience of other organizations represents the true gold mined at InterClass

This ability to learn from failure is inherent in the spirit of experimentation captured in Norm #7. Experimentation, as we know from Thomas Edison, can involve many dark failures before the bright light of success. We use the word *innovation* at the very beginning of the InterClass mission because we are committed to continuous experimentation with new approaches. InterClass often revisits topics of interest to our membership with totally new methods and materials. These norms free InterClass participants to speak up when they are unsure of something, to admit to and learn from their less-than-successful endeavors, and to be experimental within the trust-based environment of InterClass. We will look more at the importance of innovation to InterClass in later chapters.

Norm #8: Consultancies: Truthful and Thoughtful Feedback

Consultancies: truthful and thoughtful feedback is closely related to the *hard on ideas, soft on people* norm described earlier. One of the benefits of InterClass throughout its history has been the opportunity for member companies to advise each other on particularly tough and confidential issues. Later in the book, we will discuss some of the different methods used to perform these consultancies. For now, it's important to note that this norm results in truthful and thoughtful feedback to the company requesting the consultancy.

Consultancies: All participants focusing on one participant's issue

The truthful part relates to the *hard on ideas* norm. It is demonstrated by participants who willingly bring forward lessons learned from their professional and personal life. In addition to their current organizational context, participants draw on their experiences at other organizations or from the earlier stages of their career. Shared stories of personal growth often provide the most illuminating insights.

The thoughtful part of the last norm relates to the *soft on people* norm by encouraging advisors to be thoughtful in their advice to ensure it is actionable and on point. It is essential that advisors respect prior individual decisions made by the company requesting advice. Because of our high trust environment, advisors are also feel free to disclose sensitive information without feeling vulnerable or exposed.

Your Organization's Norms

We hope these "rules of the game" for InterClass provide insight into the ways we operate. We believe that most of the elements of this list would benefit most organizations. The real point, though, is that leaders need to adopt a list that best supports the mission and culture of their specific firm. Workers need to understand the rules of their organization's game—whatever they are. The more explicit a leader can make these norms, the more effective they will be at promoting the organization's health. It is the leader's duty to speak to and manage to the rules of their game. The leader must also prevent the growth of subversive norms that are adhered to, but never spoken, that can destroy the productive fabric of an organization. Leaders need to begin by honestly assessing the degree of success their organization is achieving. When something is amiss—large or small—an active examination of the "lived" norms is a part of what is needed. There are business anthropologists who specialize in helping leaders with this kind of review. However, all leaders, in large or small organizations, will learn a great deal about the "lived" norms in their organization by just placing their attention on discovering what these norms are during the everyday activities they perform themselves in meetings and walking around. The next step will be to describe the gap between the "lived" and "desired" norms. The desired norms are those that the leadership believes can best support organization success.

These norms can then be put in words through corporate communications such as vision statements, values, strategic plans, and tactical implementation documents. It does not matter which or how many of these vehicles are used. What is important is that the norms are made as explicit as possible to as many workers as possible to ensure that everyone shares a collective vision toward achieving the organization's mission. Successful organizations always have shared norms—though they may be neither explicit nor emotionally healthy. However, when they are explicit and healthy the adaptability of the organization is greatly heightened and therefore the ability of the organization to efficiently change strategy or even norms based on

Making norms healthy and explicit, and living up to them are competencies required of leaders by the increasing global changes in which all organizations operate.

major changes in the environment is heightened. At InterClass we believe that making norms healthy and explicit, and living up to them, are competencies required of leaders by the increasing global changes in which all organizations operate.

Exercise: Bringing Your Organization's Norms Into Plain Sight

This exercise is intended to help you note more of what actually happens in your organization vs. what are said to be the norms or values. Try carrying a piece of paper and note in one column the norms you see enacted and then write in the opposite column how these are similar to or different from the officially verbalized norms or values of your organization. You could use a numeric rating for adding up how aligned enacted norms are to published norms. Remember to listen for emotions, when they come up in meetings tells you a lot about what your true norms are. Do people share their thoughts frequently? Are they thanked for their ideas? Are they cut off or punished for offering criticism or new ideas? How do your observations fit with published values?

THE UNIT OF ONE

Creating Collective Value Can Only Be Accomplished By Addressing the Needs of Individuals

What this chapter is about...

InterClass believes that for group interactions to succeed—whether their purpose is to launch a new product, develop a strategy for responding to the changing global business environment, or conduct an InterClass high speed exchange—the individuals making up the group must be fully engaged. This engagement, of the whole-self, which we refer to as "being fully present," is a prerequisite and must be achieved prior to engaging in group efforts. In turn, a prerequisite for enabling each participant to be fully present is the recognition by facilitators and leaders of the complex, multi-layered uniqueness of each individual.

> *InterClass wants ALL OF YOU: the personal, the intellectual, the spiritual, the worker, and so on.*

InterClass aims to enable every participant at an InterClass event to be fully present. The more present we are, the more we contribute and the more we receive. Having each individual fully present is a key driver of the overall effectiveness of our participants, making them more productive and innovative than the mere "sum of their parts." In other words, $1+1+1+1+1 > 5$.

We also refer to this process as optimizing for "Unit of One." "Unit of One," is a term coined by *Fast Company* magazine in the 1990s to refer to "going beyond the old economy where business revolved around the organization—to a new economy where the organization revolves around the individual." Enabling "units of one" to "learn and do" was a Fast Company Mantra.[39] At InterClass, the "Unit of One" reflects our recognition that the basic "unit" of our work is not the group but each of the individuals participating in the group. Doing all we can to enable individuals to participate as freely, whole-heartedly, and trustfully as possible is our job and when we do our job well, our participants can "learn and do" more effectively. InterClass works to optimize for the full presence of each and every participant, customizing our events so that each unit of one is fully present. This is similar to the way digital technology is enabling products to be customized to individual consumers, such as Levi Strauss creating "personal pair" using a digitized version of you to enable a personal fitting for each pair of jeans. At InterClass, we use a range of methods to inspire participants to become fully present, knowing that different approaches will be needed to encourage different individuals.

Why these concepts matter to leaders...

What is true for InterClass with regard to encouraging individuals to be fully present is true for any organization. In a well-functioning organization, the more a leader can enable every member of his or her team to be fully present, the more effective the overall team will be. As with the chapter on Disengage to Engage, in this chapter on the Unit of One, we will first describe what InterClass does to optimize for each unit of one and then we will discuss how this applies to what leaders need to do in their organizations.

---

39. The Fast Company Unit of One concepts are explained at http://www.fastcompany. com/magazine/05/edpage5.html

THE UNIT OF ONE

In order to be fully present I need to be grounded in who I am and I need to know what I think.

The first attribute of being fully present is knowing who I am and working to activate that self-knowledge outwardly. It is the authentic self we are striving to bring forward. It is easy to get out of the habit of being fully present. Sometimes it is even better not to be fully present in order to protect parts of ourselves. When we are in unhealthy work environments, where the whole individual is not respected, it can be psychologically healthier to only bring parts of ourselves to the workplace. It takes intent and concentration to be fully present. At InterClass, we speak our intent, our desire, to have everyone fully present. We talk about wanting the whole person to show up at our meetings. The concept of InterClass as an oasis refers in great part to this ability not to have to parse oneself at an InterClass event. InterClass wants all of you: the personal, the intellectual, the spiritual, the worker, and so on.

Articulating our desire for all participants to be fully present is important, but it could not be realized without the corresponding behaviors of InterClass staff and participants that enable the intent to live. Leaders, too, may be explicit about wanting full presence in the work environment, but this aim will go unrealized and may even be detrimental if the leader then exhibits behavior that shuts down members of their team. This negative behavior most commonly takes the form of not respecting the words of team members. Cutting off someone's thoughts and feelings, especially when that person may be testing the waters to figure out if it's a safe space to fully contribute, and/or not providing any feedback, are both highly detrimental to getting the best from everyone. Leaders rarely act this way intentionally. Time pressures rather than disrespect may be the cause of these kinds of interruptions and silences. Establishing ground rules for how long one speaks or for the type of input sought can do much to eliminate unintentional dishonoring of co-workers' words. Many exercises used at InterClass have tight time constraints, but everyone knows what they are and understands how to get their words heard.

Techniques for Developing Concentration on Being Present

Earlier we said it takes concentration as well as intent to be fully present. At InterClass, we use several methods to improve concentration on being present by helping participants understand who they are and what they think.

Closed Eye Imagery

Closed eye imagery is a technique to help make unconscious (or at least not top-of-mind) thinking and feeling apparent to individuals. Closed eye imagery enables a group to concentrate on a particular question while having a very personal experience with their own views on the question. A question is read aloud by a facilitator. Individuals are then asked to close their eyes and imagine that they are in different locations, seeing and interacting with various objects. At certain points, participants are asked to open their eyes and write down what they 'see.' At the end of the exercise, participants are guided through the process of interpreting the meaning of the images that came to mind for them. The surfacing of unconscious or uncommon thoughts and feelings enables participants to surface significant aspects of their identity—their values, thoughts, and passions. It also deepens the nature of the conversations they have with other participants. Speaking from deeply understood thoughts, interests, and values encourages all of those in the conversation to do the same. This technique was brought to the field of business facilitation by Eric Vogt, one of the founders of InterClass, in the 1990's after he was instructed in it by Magaly, a student of Native American teachings. The deep conversations experienced with the assistance of creative imagery are the kinds of interactions we promote at InterClass. This is why we work so hard to enable each "Unit of One" to be fully present.

Brainwriting

To enable understanding of one's own thoughts, and to avoid group think (the tendency of a group to go along with the majority or leaders' opinion), we've found it's important to allow individuals time with their own thoughts before hearing the views of others. At InterClass, we often use the technique of brainwriting before we enter into any form of discussion or group brainstorming session. In brainwriting individuals write down in as spontaneous a manner as possible, their own ideas inspired by provocative words, questions or phrases voiced by a facilitator. It is essential that no interactions with others happen during this writing process. When an individual has completed their response, they are able to later reference their own ideas when listening to the ideas of others, so that their thoughts do not get lost in the thoughts of those around them. It also allows them to record the impact the words of others may have on their original idea without losing the kernel of what was unique about that idea and unique about the words used to express it.

Applying the Unit of One to the Workplace

In the workplace leaders can do a great deal to reduce the likelihood of group think and improve the comprehensiveness of the thoughts and ideas individuals bring to meetings by requesting some form of action that requires individual reflection ahead of time. The simple action of distributing agendas before a meeting inspires participants to think ahead about their views on the agenda's topics. Further actions along these lines can include asking different people to research and provide different perspectives on the question at hand. Of course, brainwriting in the room can be an efficient way to allow for individual reflection especially when a new topic comes up in the moment. However, it is far more effective, when possible, to have participants be "present" with an understanding of their own view on a question than to ask them to try to develop a view while others are trying to do the same. It's harder still when others are trying to discuss or debate the nuances of different perspectives on the topic. Being fully present requires knowing who I am and what I think.

Note Taking

A key component of being fully present is simply being awake and aware: awake in order to contribute and awake in order to receive; aware of our own and other people's requests. Participants can miss opportunities to contribute or gain insights simply because they are not aware in the moment—they are daydreaming or musing on the topic at hand or experiencing mind talk on a very different agenda. At InterClass, we always encourage note taking. Psychologists have long known the value of using note taking as a way of maintaining their concentration on what their patients are saying. Psychologists, like everyone else, may have their minds wander on occasion, especially with the eighth patient on a Friday afternoon. They have developed techniques for catching themselves at daydreaming, by looking at the last comment they noted, listening more deeply in the awakening moment, and asking the patient a question to be sure they have connected where they were to where they are. The goal here is not to prevent the mind from drifting. Wandering off in our minds can actually be of value. During these drifts some important and relevant ideas may be generated. Sometimes we need to give our minds space to let spontaneous ideas surface. Instead, the idea is to allow the drift, but then bring the mind back to what is happening in the moment, or in the case of InterClass, return to what the group is doing and saying. This process of retrieving our thoughts when they drift also provides the opportunity to capture that important reflection that occurred while your awareness was not focused on what the group was doing and saying, perhaps by creating a note to bring up later with the group.

Leaders can do much to improve awareness in their corporate cultures by encouraging note taking. The absence of note taking often occurs in organizations with trust issues—the leader views notes as something that can cause them problems later down the road. A pervasive absence of note taking in an organization can serve as an excellent bellwether of deeper concerns about presence and trust.

Pairing and the Buddy System

New participants at InterClass may have a more difficult time staying aware and awake. It is easy to get distracted by the unfamiliar or simply not be sure where it is best to place one's attention. InterClass works on this by pairing new participants with a longstanding member who helps explain and facilitate the new person's understanding of our norms and processes. This is further facilitated by our habit of always reviewing the InterClass norms at the beginning of each session. This "buddy system" is part of the InterClass guarantee to experience our Oasis from the very beginning of your involvement.

Buddy systems can be very effective in organizations as well. Leaders who concern themselves with the success of new entrants in their organizations do well to have an old master show the new kid on the block the ways of the road. This can greatly accelerate how quickly a new worker can become fully present, inculcated in an organization's processes and thus more quickly able to fully contribute.

Event Environment

At InterClass we find some of the best techniques for encouraging awareness and being awake involve the event environment. We carefully design each room for intimate conversations. This means using tables that fit only four or five people and never using theater-style environments. This is further supported by the interaction techniques used throughout InterClass events such as knowledge cafés, which support the organic sharing of ideas across large numbers of people without the use of report outs (more on the cafés in later chapters). We also vary the environment during the day, so there are times when participants will work in pairs without tables, sometimes everyone will be standing in the room with no furniture, and times for individual work involving flip charts, multi-colored markers, and paste-able art work. Change helps participants stay awake and alert, and these different physical formats support the various methodologies we use at InterClass to promote and share deep conversations. It is also important to always remember that basic comfort counts—people cannot think or communicate well in uncomfortable chairs or poorly lit rooms.

Leaders do well to remember to match environment and purpose. Much can be done to affect the mood of a team by varying the colors in a room and the type of lighting available. Awake and aware participation depends greatly on the surrounding environment. Decision-making sessions can be brought to a lull by the closing of curtains and dimming of lights for a slide show presentation. On the other hand, a vibrant room, filled with light and color, energizes participants and frees their thinking. Leaders should also consider how they are personally affected by their environment—this is just another way of being attentive to their own "Unit of One." This "selfish" awareness can enable leaders to insure that their own moods and productivity have the power to motivate those around them. Environment—whether we are talking about ergonomics or energy enhancement—can offer a great deal of insurance toward achieving full presence and thus, provide the conditions for an effective meeting or for enhancement of one's own productivity.

CREATING THE "WE SPACE"

Participants, now more present in themselves,
together create a safe environment for sharing & learning

What this chapter is about...

"We Space" refers to the time we spend at InterClass events:

- exchanging ideas
- opening ourselves to new concepts
- identifying blinders we may have to particular points of view
- inventing totally new concepts
- making comparisons between our differing perspectives

In other words, it's where we do most of our learning, the place where old assumptions are surfaced, and where new insights and creative combinations occur.

Why "We Space" is important...

Establishing the "We Space" is what we spend most of our time on at InterClass—it's the heart of what we do. Essentially, the "We Space" is our learning model. It's composed of four separate processes, as follows:

- Developing and articulating perspectives
- Sharing and refining perspectives

- Surfacing our assumptions and mental models
- Absorbing new content and practicing potential actions

Over the years, we've found that "We Space" is most reliably achieved when participants have first disengaged from where they have been so that they are free to engage where they are. It is also a pre-requisite to arriving at "We Space" that the needs of each participant, each "Unit of One," has been met. If you've been reading this book sequentially, you're already familiar with the concepts of disengage to engage and the "Unit of One." We do try to move participants through these processes in this sequence. But, as should be evident by now, the different phases of the InterClass process don't always occur in this order. Sometimes we need to cycle back and work on disengaging more than once during an event. Sometimes a topic lends itself to more individual work, at the "Unit of One" level. In general, though, we need to attend to disengagement and individualization before we are ready to move into the "We Space."

We need to attend to disengagement and individualization before we are ready to move into the "We Space."

What are the implications for leaders?

Talent is perhaps the most important asset in today's knowledge economy, and creating "We Space" can help you get the most from the talent in your organization. The ability of a CEO to lead talent correlates strongly to the overall success of her organization. Successful talent management and employee development requires characteristics that InterClass is fortunate to be able to take for granted, like engagement and commitment to purpose. Only the engaged and the committed show up at InterClass sessions. But many employees show up for work in body—not in mind or spirit. An organization with engaged employees, among other things, provides support to help their employees feel competent in their roles. Corporate leaders who understand that they need to develop and reinforce employee competence are ahead of the game when it comes to organizational success. Reinforcing what employees do well ensures that they will continue these positive behaviors. So often we focus more on what we see that is wrong, despite all the data on appreciative feedback demonstrating its greater effectiveness. This is why at InterClass we work at techniques such as appreciative inquiry, an approach to personal and organizational change grounded in affirmation and appreciation of the positive. Appreciative inquiry techniques promote human communications that enable people to shift their focus from problems to "productive possibilities for the future."[40]

Groundwork

There are initial levels of employee competence that leaders need to focus on before enhancing the skills and knowledge needed by the organization. The first level refers to the competence of an individual to develop a personal perspective on the mission, strategy, and values of the organization and an understanding of how their role fits in the strategy and the organization's probability of success. In the Corporate Leadership Council's work on engagement, presented by Dirk Petersen of CLC at an InterClass session called Full Engagement, this concept was reinforced by two of the top five levers of engagement identified by CLC. These were:

- connection between work and organizational strategy
- importance of job to organizational success

These levers also represent another key descriptor of an initial competence, which is the ability to contribute to the thinking of the community. Once I understand my place in the organization, I can begin to contribute with ideas and by molding my actions and efforts to enhance the efforts of my team, department, and company. Only after first developing a personal perspective on the organization and their place in it are employees then able to reach the level of competence required for their company's success. As we long ago discovered at InterClass, starting with group activities "We Space" without allowing each participant to first develop or review their own perspective results in inarticulate, incomplete interactions and greater susceptibility to group think. Once this "Unit of One" perspective is developed, leaders need to help employees move on to the primary focus of "We Space" in the work environment—their

---

competence at performing their work. This competence is again indicated among the top five levers of engagement identified by CLC as, employees understanding how to complete work projects

We've seen how the "Unit of One" contributes to the effectiveness of the individual at an InterClass event and at work. Let's now look at how the "We Space" moves people from individual to organizational competence. To reiterate, at InterClass, we've identified four key processes that are needed to achieve "We Space":

- Developing perspectives
- Sharing and refining perspectives
- Surfacing assumptions and mental models and
- Absorbing content and practicing actions

We will now look in turn at the multiple methods used to deliver each of these processes.

InterClass' Four Key Processes to Achieving "We Space" Process 1: Developing Perspectives

Powerful Questions

The first step in achieving "We Space" is creating a place in which participants can develop and articulate their individual perspectives. First, we create the conditions to enable all participants (the *we* of "We Space") to reach a basic level of competence on the topic at hand. By *competence*, we mean that each participant develops a personal point of view and an understanding of what they still need to learn about a topic. It also means that each participant is

Competence: Developing a personal point of view, an understanding of what one still needs to learn about a topic, and readiness to contribute to the development of a community perspective.

at a point where he or she can contribute to the development of a community—or InterClass—perspective on the topic.

Our participants tend to arrive with open minds. They may hold a perspective on the topic at hand, but we offer them every encouragement to loosen their hold on that viewpoint so that new and innovative concepts can influence everyone's perspective. InterClass employs a great number of techniques to do this, many of which are based in a body of work known as powerful questions begun over 15 years ago by Eric Vogt, the CEO of InterClass.[41]

A powerful question:

- generates energy and a motivation to explore
- is "thought-provoking"
- stimulates reflective thinking
- challenges or alters assumptions
- channels inquiry, promises insight
- is compelling and enduring
- touches a deeper meaning
- evokes more questions.

Powerful questions are generative, that is, they grow us in new directions. They help us break out of our cognitive ruts so we can explore more fertile ground. They enable us to shift our focus so we can see old things in new ways, and see new things for the first time.

So, how do we create powerful questions? Three factors affect the power of a question:

- its *scope* (what and how much the question covers)
- its *construction* (the language used to frame the question)
- its *context* (the setting in which the question resides)

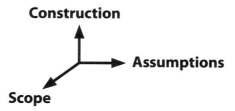

Generally, the larger its *scope*, the more powerful the question is perceived to be. Think of how different it feels when you are asked at a

---

41. Vogt, Eric E. Brown, Juanita, and Issacs, David. (2003) *The Art of Powerful Questions: Insight, Innovation and Art.* Pegasus Communication..

meeting, "If we implement this strategy, how might we affect our region?" versus "How might we affect the planet?" There is a limit here though. You must make sure that the scope described is credible to the nature of the problem. Asking "How might today's meeting affect the universe?" is probably not a credible question for many audiences. In general, though, increasing a question's scope from an immediate concern with the here and now to a broader domain and a longer time horizon will almost always raise its power.

The *construction* of a question influences its power by limiting or expanding the range of potential responses. Yes/no and either/or questions are closed-response questions—they can generate only two potential responses. In such questions, the content and structure of the response are predetermined by the originating question. But interrogative questions (those that ask *how, what,* or *why*) have an infinite number of potential responses—they require reflection both about the content and the construction of a response.

A yes/no question might ask, "Are you satisfied with our working relationship?" To reply, I need only reflect on my feelings and say yes or no. To notch the power of the question up a bit, you might ask: "When have you been satisfied with our working relationship?" Now I have to reflect on specific events and times; I have to think in terms of stories. My response now needs to provide examples and context. The question becomes even more powerful when asked, "What is it about our working relationship that you find most satisfying?" Now I am being asked to supply a description of "most satisfying" so I need to reflect on comparisons, while still providing stories and examples. Going one level higher would be achieved by asking, "Why might it be that our working relationship has had its ups and downs?" Now I am being asked to reflect on causality, and not on one condition, but on at least two—our relationship's ups and downs.

As you can see in the above examples, different interrogatives (when, what, why) have differing degrees of power. Across most cultures, people create a hierarchy of interrogatives that looks like:

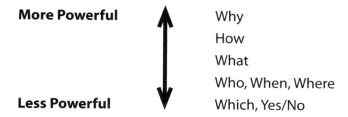

Leaders need to welcome and encourage fresh questions and open minds in all their associates. Dr. Elizabeth Watson of Stevens Institute of Technology conducted a business anthropology study of two different organizations to investigate how their leadership ran meetings. The quality of the decisions and the level of creativity in Organization A, which encouraged individual perspectives and challenged each others' points of view, was far greater than in Organization B, which had a formal meeting structure where most of the talking was done by the top leadership and few public challenges occurred.

InterClass leverages powerful questions in its sessions continuously. They are at work in the Creative Imagery exercise we presented in the previous chapter, *The Unit of One*. The facilitator poses a powerful question to spur each participant to generate creative images. The success/value of this exercise depends on the amount of power in the focusing question. If it motivates exploration and stimulates reflection, we know it has done its job.

High-Speed Exchanges

We also use powerful questions in our high speed exchanges, the InterClass method of preparing and presenting materials to allow participants to rapidly and effectively absorb a broad array of key knowledge points about the required subject. A common purpose for these exchanges when they are used in the InterClass consulting practice is to establish an appropriate base of knowledge in an organization prior to undertaking some form of strategic change.

These exchanges begin with seminal literature relevant to the topic at hand; InterClass synthesizes the present and historic viewpoints while surfacing leading edge thinking. High speed exchanges cover multiple authors, in multiple media, over multiple timeframes. The goal is to depict a comprehensive view of a field. In today's business world, where participants are experiencing ever increasing demands on their time, high speed exchanges enable participants to gain exposure to new thinking and varied perspectives without needing to immerse themselves in a time-consuming identification, prioritization and summarization of a multi-faceted and large body of work. The InterClass high speed exchange does it for them.

Susan Saltrick, a member of the InterClass staff, has been pivotal in honing and presenting our high speed exchanges in recent years. Prior to her arrival, this role was played by different experts in the field under study. Susan, an expert in education and a high-order practitioner of the art of synthesis, has effectively eliminated any concerns about the Exchanges "stacking the deck" with the views of a single expert. We strive for objectivity and inclusiveness in every high speed exchange.

In addition to synthesizing a significant volume of materials (that would take participants days of time on their own to identify, never mind read and analyze), InterClass designs interactive conversations, games, simulations, and sharable documentation to ensure the timely acquisition of the knowledge needed.

Before commissioning a high speed exchange, the InterClass design team will spend significant reflective time composing the questions it wants addressed in the review. Doing this keeps the scope of the Exchange to a manageable level and ensures that participants (as represented by design team members) care deeply about exploring the questions selected.

These questions go from opening questions—questions one would ask when beginning to learn about a new field (e.g., What is a business model?)—to more powerful questions requiring considerable reflection (e.g., Why is a business model characterized as emerging?). By varying the power of the questions used to focus the high speed exchanges we are able to promote the development of perspectives among our participants, whether they have only a little background in the topic or a great deal, enabling everyone to contribute to the thinking of the entire community.

Leaders in organizations have less and less time to consider history. It's a cliché, but a true one—if we do not pay attention to history, we are bound to repeat it. Organizations that have methods for reviewing prior actions and reviving earlier learning are better able to leverage the lessons of the past and avoid its pitfalls.

Examples of exchanges performed by the InterClass consulting practice to help organizations leverage lessons from the recent past include

- developing a synthesis of historical and present thinking on what brand marketing is all about for a global consumer products organization moving from a multi- to a unified-brand identity
- creating a synthesis of present thinking on the global economy to heighten the understanding of a financial services organization moving into international markets
- building a picture of consensus and diversity of critical success factors identified by major pundits in the field of mergers and acquisitions to support a financial services organization going into a merger of peers.

Recent high speed exchanges for our multi-client practice have covered topics such as

- Emerging business models
- Customer engagement
- Sustainability and
- Characteristics of a 21st century workforce

The questions, generated by the design team, that spurred the emerging business models high speed exchange were

- What is a business model?
- Why is a business model characterized as emerging?
- What enables a business model to be sustaining?
- What is the product, operating method, and culture exemplified by this business model?
- How does each model describe success?
- What is the leadership style of each organization surveyed?
- What are the similarities and differences among organizations characterized as having emerging business models?

Appreciative Inquiry

The third technique we use at InterClass to develop perspectives is appreciative inquiry, or AI. AI is a technique first developed by David Cooperider at Case Western University, and now employed across the globe in an astonishing variety of situations—from conflict resolution to business planning, from negotiating differences between hostile nations to family therapy and community activism. Its title effectively says what it is—asking questions (inquiring) using positive, appreciative language. Most appreciative inquiries begin with the simple question, "What is working well around here?" It may seem easy, but most people find using positive language throughout the entire process takes incredible discipline. Appreciative inquiry is based on the notion that you make things better by looking at what's right about a relationship, a contract, a workplace, rather than wallowing in what makes things wrong. In fact, appreciative inquiry asserts that focusing attention on what is wrong emphasizes the negative and prolongs the pain that people are in.

Appreciative inquiry has four levels:

1. **Discovery**—establishing an inquiry of the positive
2. **Dream**—creating actionable vision grounded in the potential of what has been discovered
3. **Design**—creating possibilities that will surpass the discovered potential
4. **Destiny**—furthering hope and momentum in service of the higher vision

At InterClass we develop perspectives through use of the discovery component—by framing questions from a positive "what's working well here?" perspective.

Wisdom Council

A fourth method we use at InterClass to develop perspectives comes from Wind Eagle and Rainbow Hawk of the Ehama Institute, authors of *Heart Seeds, a Message from the Ancestors*. We have been privileged over the years to have them run a wisdom council for the InterClass membership. In Native American practice, chiefs of various tribes would gather from time to time to deal with issues of great importance to their people. Each leader at the table was required to represent a particular perspective—a point of view that was assigned to them, rather than the one they held. Through this creative act of speaking from the point of view of another, the chiefs were able to soften the hard edges of their differences and find common wisdom to resolve their issues. We have learned from the Council process to make sure that all possible perspectives have been considered on a particular topic/question. Sometimes we ask participants to espouse a position different from their own in order to bring that perspective into the room. By applying another lens, our view of the situation shifts, and we can envision new ways of being.

A culture of respect is essential for engagement to occur. Leaders need to observe what perspectives are not being represented in their meetings and decision-making processes. Missing perspectives can be as damaging to an organization as having the wrong one. Diversity of views, though, promotes the identification of potential pitfalls in strategic thinking, tactical analysis, and daily decisions. By inviting differing perspectives into the process, whether that involves functional diversity or diversity of thinking styles or life experience, leaders can feel more assured of the comprehensiveness of their decisions. This is also supported by the research of CLC on engagement, where one of the top five levers of employee engagement is that the "company demonstrates a strong commitment to diversity."

Process 2: Sharing and Refining Perspectives

Once individuals discover and articulate their own perspectives, we encourage them to share and refine those perspectives collectively. To do this, we use three primary techniques:

- Knowledge cafés
- Journaling
- "Have You Considered?"

Several of these techniques can be used for other objectives as well and are also addressed in other parts of this book.

The knowledge café

Knowledge cafés are guided by a set of operating principles. First, we create hospitable space—people think best and share most easily when they are comfortable and relaxed. Second, we make sure the questions under exploration are powerful ones—ones that really matter to the group. Next, we connect diverse people and ideas—creative friction and differing views make for richer exchange and more fruitful innovation. We encourage each person to contribute and share—by moving around the room from table to table, everyone's voice can be heard. We also listen together for patterns, insights, and deeper questions. Finally, we use various techniques to make the collective knowledge visible.

Knowledge cafés, developed in conjunction with Juanita Brown and David Isaacs of the World café, are among the most beloved techniques InterClass uses. knowledge cafés were created out of the belief that:

- Networks are the underlying pattern of living systems
- Compelling questions encourage collective learning
- The future is born in human conversation
- Intelligence emerges when a group connects in diverse and creative ways
- Collectively, we have access to all the wisdom and resources we need.

Through a knowledge café, we can mobilize the wisdom of the group without resorting to tired group processes like small team discussions, and lengthy report outs to the plenary group. A knowledge café is a process of accelerated knowledge generation and exchange that can be used for groups ranging in size from twelve to twelve hundred. The core of the technology is ancient—the café table, which seats four people engaged in an intimate conversation. The knowledge café starts with powerful questions and flows with the energy of the participants towards innovative perspectives and collective insight.

The best way to appreciate a knowledge café is to participate in one, but we'll try our best to give you a feel for it by providing detailed instructions. Like most elegant technologies, knowledge cafés are pretty simple in their implementation. The setup, facilitation, and debrief of a knowledge café is important, though. We've developed the following guidelines to help:

Set Up

Use one-meter round café tables if at all possible. You should have one table for every four participants.

- Try not to have too many empty tables. This helps create the sense of social space. You want to create a feeling of a sociable, lively room—like a party full of people.
- Have exactly four chairs per table. (The number four is very important!)
- Recreate the atmosphere of a café. The context creates the mood of exploration and creativity. Checkered table cloths. Jazz music. Color.
- Have large flipchart paper on the tables so that participants can make notes, sketches, and doodles to illustrate and illuminate their thoughts. Provide multiple colored markers that work!
- Dim the lights and serve tea and coffee.

Facilitation

- Begin with a few powerful questions that have been constructed by the group themselves. These can be evoked collectively through the powerful questions process. Or, you can have each person write a question on a Post-it note and paste it to their nametag. Then, everyone moves about the room to find three other people who are asking a similar question.

- Have four people per table. (Four people is magical. NOT five, but do accept three if the size of your overall group requires it.)

- Each table selects a question and dives into generative conversation. If you have more than one question, let each table self-select the questions in the priority in which they feel most energized. Don't worry, all the questions usually get covered because of the diversity of interests in a room. And, if any items do not get covered, that too is a useful demonstration of the overall group's true assessment of that question's relevance.

- Ask people to consciously listen three times more than they talk. Encourage them to draw pictures of the conversation, the ideas, and insights.

- Minimum 25 minutes, maximum 45 minutes per round. Timing the rounds is where you, the facilitator, earn your keep. Circulate, listen to conversations, look at the pictures, and notice body language. Allow sufficient time for the conversation to bubble and pop, but end the round before the energy sputters out.

- At the end of the round, ring a bell. At each table, one host remains, while the three other people move to new, and, where possible, separate tables.

- At the beginning of the new round, the table host welcomes the three new conversation partners, and explains the perspective generated so far. (The drawings and doodles on the paper will help with this.) New table partners also summarize the conversation from their former tables.

- Then encourage the conversation to flow naturally from there, following the interests of the new foursome, and building on the insights generated in the previous round(s). Remember, learning is a social process.

- At the end of three or four rounds most people in the room will have heard the ideas generated by the others in the café, and will have had a chance to integrate them into an emerging collective sense of meaning and momentum. There is NO NEED for one-on-one time consuming report outs from each table.

Debrief

When the conversational rounds are complete, you'll want to make the emerging collective meaning visible. We do this through a number of techniques depending upon the number of participants, amount of energy in the room, and whether this is a terminal exercise on the topic or something that will spill over into the next day or a follow-up event via the web. Here are some of the techniques in our debriefing portfolio:

- **Journaling**: We often ask each individual to journal their insights and their implications onto a single summary page of insights. We then collect those pages, and synthesize the individual summaries into a collective view which we distribute back to the group by the next gathering time.

- **Imaging**: When we sense there's a strong desire to see the collective view immediately, we may debrief the insights rapidly—sometimes asking participants to draw pictures that encapsulate their learning.

- **Affinity Exercises**: We sometimes ask participants to put their thoughts and conclusions on Post-it notes during a knowledge café. Then we ask only a few participants from different café tables to group the Post-its. The Post-its from all of the tables are collected and then grouped around similar ideas and/or patterns. This process enables broader patterns and the strength of collective wisdom to emerge.

- **Circle Dialogue**: Sometimes it is most effective to simply have a large circle dialogue. We borrow the Native American tradition of using a talking stick, which is passed around the circle. The person holding the stick reflects briefly on the most meaningful insight from the café on the highest priority for action. Then they pass the stick to the person sitting to their right and so on, until everyone around the circle has spoken. One or two note takers record what is said and then synthesize the results for dissemination the following day.

Knowledge cafés are a wonderful method for both sharing and refining perspectives. Virtually every participant feels empowered through sharing their views in a knowledge café. They find they can hone their own perspectives to a high level of refinement. Consistently, we find participants deeply engage with the knowledge café process. How could they not? They have 20 conversations on a topic they care about with other equally passionate people, all within the space of two hours!

We get requests for instructions on running a knowledge café from inside companies more than any other technique we use. These requests have come from senior staff such as country mangers and heads of marketing of *Fortune 500* companies. Here, then, is a very direct recommendation for leaders. The quality with which you share and refine ideas directly impacts the quality of the decisions made. We know no better process than knowledge café to share and refine perspectives. This too is supported by one of the top five levers of engagement identified by CLC: effective internal communication.

Journaling

We've seen how journaling can be used while debriefing a knowledge café. We've also found it to be a wonderful stand-alone technique for refining ideas at the individual ("Unit of One") level before sharing and further refining individual views with the group. To show how important we feel journaling is, we'll often provide participants with a beautiful book that demonstrates respect for their notes, doodles, and drawings. We'll often print the powerful questions we are examining right in the book as reinforcement. Some people prefer journaling to speaking and feel they produce their most refined insights through these exercises.

Astute leaders are aware that their people have varying verbal styles—some love to take the stage, some prefer to express themselves more privately. By encouraging note-taking and the sharing of information in writing as well as verbally, leaders increase the likelihood that their company will get the very best thinking from the widest diversity of their employees.

Have You Considered…?

One of our favorite sharing and refining exercises, developed in conjunction with a global consumer goods company, is called "Have you considered." It, too, is a very simple and elegant technique, with very few steps required for its implementation. We use "Have you considered" to conduct peer consultancies—that is, sessions in which the network focuses its collective wisdom on a critical business issue raised by one participant organization. The process begins when the group, gathered in a circle, listens as one participant raises a business concern or opportunity. Two other participants have volunteered to take notes. Then, in "popcorn" fashion— speaking up as soon as an idea pops into one's head—participants offer ideas and suggestions about the issue. Their comments must start with the words, "Have you considered...?" and must be limited to a single sentence.

The member listens without comment and then simply says, "thank you" in response to each idea. Either party can request clarification if something is really not understood, but other than that communication is limited to the format stated above. The person raising the issue is thus unable to say things like, "Oh, we tried that last year" or "How am I going to get the money to do that?" The effect of this positive affirmation of ideas is miraculous. Like appreciative inquiry, amazing things can happen when the focus is on the positive. Most issues are covered in about five minutes—and the number of ideas generated is astounding. Pages upon pages are recorded by the note takers. In our experience, everyone who participates feels appreciated. The ideas keep getting more reflective and thoughtful as the process continues, and the virtuous circle just keeps getting bigger.

Process 3: Surfacing Assumptions and Mental Models

We've looked at a number of ways we develop and surface our individual perspectives. Once those individual views have been made visible, we are then able to examine them more critically. The next step in creating the "We Space" is to surface assumptions and mental models that are operating at both individual and collective levels. Our assumptions and mental models, especially when they are not conscious or overt, can get in the way of our being able to change our perspective or our ways of behaving. InterClass is all about gathering new insights—we do all that we can to ensure that the emerging perspectives aren't subverted by participants' own unconscious assumptions.

Mental Models

As Peter Senge wrote in his best-seller, *The Fifth Discipline*, "Mental models are deeply ingrained assumptions, generalizations, or even pictures or images that influence how we understand the world and how we take action. Very often, we are not consciously aware of our mental models or the effects they have on our behavior."[42] Mental models can help us streamline our responses and thus promote efficiency, but they can lead us astray as well. Mental models are shaped by our perceptions—by the patterns we think we see. Over time, this pattern recognition can become a rut, though, and we can mistakenly think we recognize a situation as being just like an earlier one, when in fact, it's quite a different thing. Thus, mental models need to be surfaced from time to time to keep our perceptions fresh and our responses keen.

Working with the mental models held by individuals is a particularly delicate business, and so the InterClass operating principle of "hard on ideas, soft on people" becomes especially important. Because mental models are often unconsciously and vigorously held, it is important to be gentle on the person doing the holding. Just as with appreciative inquiry, it takes real discipline and craft to communicate this soft intention. Skilled facilitation is key to surfacing mental models and assumptions. We aim to facilitate the realization by participants of their own mental models versus participants surfacing the mental models of other participants. One of the most effective ways of doing this is to use techniques like the Ehama Institutes' Wisdom Council discussed earlier in this chapter. Methods like this encourage participants to try on new assumptions and make their own assumptions visible and more pliable through inward comparison. In a wisdom council each participant is asked to take on a particular role such as a chief of war, In a wisdom council each participant is asked to take a particular role such as a chief of war, who reminds us that emotions bring great power when they are accessible and great danger when they become stuck. War chiefs are totally flexible in their emotions. Or

42. Senge, Peter. (1990). *The Fifth Discipline*, p. 8.

another example of a role would be a chief of the hunter worker, a chief who takes on the role of creating the strategies and plans for taking action.

This process works particularly well for surfacing mental models when participants are asked to play roles UNLIKE themselves. So the war chief would ideally be played by the person perceived as fundamentally rigid in their beliefs and inflexible in their planning and the Chief of the hunter worker would be played by someone perceived as relying on their emotions in their decision making. Other ways we surface mental models at InterClass include facilitators modeling a particular line of thinking, pointing out how a mental model exists behind it, and its potential impact and outcomes. Again, having facilitators rather than participants do the modeling enables participants to identify mental models in themselves versus other participants identifying their models for them. This method relies on another concept popularized by Peter Senge—systems thinking. Systems thinking is a holistic approach to analysis that focuses on the relationship among the component parts of a system, and on changes to the system over time and within the operation of even larger systems. By illustrating the systems effect of a mental model over time we often make the model visible and the unintended and often undesirable outcomes of the model apparent. Again the goal is always to do this by enabling self-diagnosis versus any form of outside criticism.

Case Study from InterClass Consulting:
Systems Thinking Aids Global Pharmaceutical Company

Using systems thinking approaches is essential in surfacing mental models operating collectively within the cultures of our organizations. For example, for decades the pharmaceutical industry has thought of physicians as their customers. Government activity on the regulation of healthcare, the increasing power of patient organizations, organizations of health professionals, and disease-focused enterprises, such as the American Heart Association, are all factors that have dramatically changed the customer landscape for the pharmaceutical industry. In a series of dedicated sessions with a global pharmaceutical company, InterClass helped generate a new mental model for changing the definition of customer from physician to a broad group of stakeholders. First we worked with the client to design a process that enabled the identification and prioritization of a wide array of stakeholders. Going from a single customer category to over a dozen major customer categories was a daunting prospect. Developing the analytic tools to prioritize and focus activities was an essential step in breaking with the historic customer model. The next step in the process was to draw the new system that demonstrated how different parts of the company would now need to serve and influence the newly defined stakeholders. Again all of the exercises used enabled the organization and its associates to identify their own assumptions, mental models, and barriers to understanding and embracing the new customer model.

Blindness to mental models and assumptions is a pervasive condition. We recommend that leaders have periodic check-ups for themselves and their organizations to be sure to surface these models and the behavioral impacts they are having. It is best if this check-up can be performed by an outsider. This would include an executive coach on the individual level and a business anthropologist or organization behavioralist on the company level. It is like a medical check-up—you need expert equipment like x-rays and experts like doctors to be sure of what is really going on inside.

Process 4: Absorbing Content and Practicing Actions

The final stage of the "We Space" involves absorbing content so it can be applied back on the job. InterClass offers a safe space for both absorbing knowledge and practicing implementation. We've developed some fun ways to learn new content, including specially designed card games. An example is our work with Global Trends.

In the past year, InterClass developed an overview of Global Trends created from a synthesis of the work of futurists, journalists, and topical pundits on specific global issues such as energy. To enable participants to prioritize what in these future trends was important to their organizations we developed a priority setting card game. Participants in this card game got a chance to absorb the trends, by reading them from the cards and discussing them with their table groups. The card game also supported them in considering how these trends might apply to their own work environments by prioritizing the trends and describing or defending why the outcome of this trend would be critical to their business and how it would impact their actions. We have played this game both in cross-company and company dedicated sessions. Interestingly, in cross-company sessions we saw greater depth in absorbing content, and in company dedicated sessions there was a greater opportunity to practice actions indicated by the trends.

Simulations are another method for gaining new content knowledge and playing out potential actions. In a session called "The Cultural Dilemma in Mergers, Acquisitions and Alliances," we were privileged to have Brian Helweg-Larsen of Professional Skills Training create a kinetic learning experience for us. With a theme of "the merging of opposites," this simulation enabled participants to absorb at an experiential level common cultural errors encountered during mergers. In this case, when the profit-hungry traders of Upstairs Inc. encountered the quality-conscious analyzers from the Downstairs Institute, the proposed merger fell into disarray. In just a matter of hours, participants began to assume passionately held new identities. This led to a discussion about the nature of integrating cultures. What works best to integrate cultures? Taking joint action? Thinking and talking in the same time and space? If we take action together, do we integrate faster because we construct shared experiences? If we focus on thinking and talking together, do we only examine worldviews and reinforce our cultures and mental models while talking?

The simulation revealed an important fact: listening among groups was not evident during the simulation. With all the activity around the merger, this essential skill—of listening and talking across groups—had been overlooked. People dove into action and never talked about what the new values, skills, and experiences meant to them. Participants in this simulation reported significantly greater success in their later merger endeavors because of the insights they gained in this exercise.

Leaders need to be able to play games and use simulations on a companywide level. They are powerful tools for preparing a workforce for broad scale change. Simulations and games allow employees to try out the future and gain a sense of control over their professional choices.

TAKING ACTION

What this chapter is about...

At InterClass we believe strongly in applying the 80-20 rule[43] to taking action. In short, we endorse the view that it is most effective to spend 80% of your time on planning and only 20% on actually doing. The steps described in the previous chapter on "We Space" such as developing, sharing, and refining perspectives are all essential components of planning. Even the early stages of action taking are really planning focused. In the period right before action, two preliminary stages occur.

We believe it is most EFFECTIVE to spend 80% of your time on planning and only 20% on actually doing.

These are:

- Reaching consensus on actions to take
- Making preparations to take action.

While an InterClass session may inspire action in any one of the many domains of a participant's life, the critical actions InterClass focuses on are those taken by our participants in the context of their everyday

---

43. The 80-20 rule, also known as the Pareto Principle states that for many events 80% of the effects come from 20% of the potential causes.

work lives. Within the structure of an InterClass event, actions are taken that enable subsequent actions back at work. Therefore, in this chapter we will be discussing action at three different levels:

- How we take action in an InterClass session
- How our participants take action on the job based on the work we do in an InterClass session
- How leaders initiate action.

Implications for Leaders…

Action is a god among today's leaders. "The faster I can do, the more I can do" is their cheer. The quality of actions may not always be served by this emphasis of doing more, faster. We believe that it may not even support speed. Moving fast without planning can lead to costly and time-consuming revisions or unanticipated negative consequences. insuring planning occurs, even in short pre-action 15-minute "did we forget anything" sessions saves time and cost. At InterClass, we focus on planning as a quality decision-making and acceleration tool. This chapter will talk about how we achieve this in InterClass sessions and how our participants balance action and planning on the job and the essence of these examples will be applied to the leaders' role.

Preparing for Action

Peer Consultancies

As we noted, before we actually take action, we prepare for it. At our events, our participants use the method of peer consultancies to prepare for taking action on the job. We have also used these consultancies as a method to inform us about InterClass organizational strategies, such as membership outreach. The many peer consultancies we've conducted over the years fall into three major categories:

- A Peer Consultancy Presentation followed by Q&A period
- An On-Site Day
- A *Have You Considered…?* Exercise.

The first step in a peer consultancy is when a participant declares they have an opportunity or a problem related to the conference domain that they would like to explore with the InterClass community. In the early years of InterClass, participants identified a peer consultancy issue well in advance of the session and prepared handout materials and presentations for the other members. The presentations provided excellent overviews of the issue at hand. Over time, though, we noted that the feedback session that followed the presentation sometimes resulted in defensiveness or unintentional rejection of ideas. We could see this happening when the presenter noted that members' suggestions had already been tried or when other participants disputed some portion of the presentation based on their experience in their often very different organizations.

We learned from these experiences, and so sought methods that would discourage defensiveness. Our search resulted in two additional peer consultancy methods: one that focused on fast-paced feedback in the moment and the other that allowed for an even greater depth of analysis by participants before feedback was provided.

Have You Considered?

The fast-paced process we call *Have You Considered...?* (which is described in greater detail in Chapter 3) is a process that cultivates an appreciative outlook and results in a multi-page list of non-judgmental ideas that the requesting member can delve through at leisure. The participant requesting the consultancy responds to all ideas with "Thank you." Nothing else and nothing more. The focus is on capturing as many ideas as possible in a short period of time. This method eliminates any need to comment on, defend, or react to the ideas offered.

On-Site Day

The more in-depth process we have evolved towards is an on-site day. This type of consultancy is primarily available to the host of a conference or another participant organization located near the host site. In this scenario, a subset of the conference participants—generally two to five people—arrive at the conference a day ahead of time.

Participants choose to make this investment of time for varied reasons including:

- They are working on a similar problem in their own organizations, and the consultancy opens new possibilities for them
- Reciprocity (they want participants to do an on-site day for their organization)
- Desire to practice their consulting skills
- Interest in understanding the organization of a fellow member or participant in greater depth.

The small multi-company consulting team gets to examine the opportunity or problem first hand. After the on-site day, the team provides the participants at the larger InterClass event with a summary on the nature of the problem or opportunity and what they discovered. The summary also delineates their recommendations. The team members then ask their peers in the room to comment on their methods, observations, and recommendations. Again, notes are taken by InterClass staff and provided later to the requesting company for their review. But the highest value is usually delivered during the conversation between the host of the consultancy, the small team that spent the day on site, and the entire pool of participants. The focus in this consultancy method is on the multi-company consulting team. The host is not responding nor defending, and the depth and uniqueness of the results of a daylong on-site consultancy highly support a generative and appreciative conversation with all participants.

When a company volunteers for a peer consultancy, they also commit to provide feedback on what they actually implemented. They come back to an InterClass session a year or more later and deliver a presentation on their results. This presentation covers:

- What happened
- What went right
- What they would like to do differently the next time
- What they would like additional feedback about.

This enables the requesting organization to continue its work over a prolonged period and continue receiving help from the InterClass community to prepare for the actions they are choosing to take.

An Example of an InterClass Consultancy

Recently, one of our members, a major consumer goods firm, asked for help with its global project management effort. After producing an initial synthesis of relevant literature, InterClass convened a high speed exchange (described in detail in Chapter 3) attended by a group of members and friends near the member's headquarters for a 1½ -day on-site consultancy. Those gathered included representatives from a wide range of organizations, including a pharmaceutical company, a car manufacturer, a telecommunications firm, and the educational field. Together they helped the consumer goods firm uncover a deeply rooted corporate assumption that had been knocking their strategy off course. They also helped their hosts reconceptualize and rebrand the effort as global *leadership*. The re-launched project led to greater success in globalizing existing offerings and better leveraging of talent within the firm worldwide.

Other Preparing for Action Techniques

Closed Eye Imagery

We also use closed eye creative imagery, mentioned before in the "Unit of One" chapter, as a method to uncover what is missing in our action plans or what else participants want to learn about. It is a way of getting the unconscious to help us discover what our conscious minds may have glossed over.

Systems Thinking

We also use systems thinking exercises to examine the implications of different plans of action. Our participants have found these techniques to be particularly useful in considering the implications of particular actions on their constituencies, such as entire supply chains, external stakeholders, or employees and their families. Here's an example: Two of the easiest things to know about any action considered are the present state and the end goal. InterClass begins a simple systems thinking exercise with these two states at opposite ends of a piece of paper. Participants then proceed to fill in some of the most likely actions in between the two and what their consequences are likely to be. We have used these kinds of exercises on both actions being proposed for future implementation as well as on historic actions that have similarities to actions being proposed.

Systems Analysis of Toyota Factory Fire, with Bob Wolf of Boston Consulting Group

When this sort of thinking is applied to past history, we have the most complete opportunity to display all the conditions and outcomes in the system because all of the ramifications of the case are known. For example, we have on several occasions had the opportunity to have Bob Wolf, formerly of the Boston Consulting Group, share his insights with us about such occurrences as the Linux phenomenon and the Toyota-supplier factory fire that destroyed all production capacity the company had for making automatic brake valves.[44] The story in the later case involves the Toyota policy of single sourcing for efficiency leading to a complete loss of capacity in a critical part because of the destruction of the relevant plant by fire. Toyota's supply chain produced exceptionally well under these conditions, giving up intellectual capital everywhere in the supply chain and producing the critical part at the most unlikely positions in the chain.

In reviewing this case, our participants documented the positive outcomes generated by each instance of sharing information, each performance of exemplary competence in the supply chain, and the application of extreme generosity in compensation by Toyota. Then, by comparison, our participants drew after each positive occurrence what other behaviors might have been possible and what those activities might have caused. It was very clear to see this system in full operation in hindsight. While it's harder to do with an untried action, the task is easier after an exercise like the Toyota fire has been played through.

In another systems-thinking exercise, participants are asked to first diagram all important constituencies involved in a business or personal

---

44. Harvard Business Review, "How Toyota and Linux Keep Collaboration Simple", by Philip Evans & Bob Wolf, August 1, 2005 http://hbswk.hbs.edu/archive/4928.html

matter, and then indicate all the possible outcomes their actions might have on each constituency. We often go to another level by asking participants to perform this exercise more than once. This enables the identification of implications for those who influence their direct constituencies and other subtleties of operation that a single "loop" through the system will not uncover. As we will discuss further in Chapter 5, post-conference, systems thinking exercises can be done at levels of incredible depth in multiple rounds, involving large numbers of people, but even simple exercises performed by individuals can significantly open minds to previously undiscovered mental models. These exercises are a wonderful tool for avoiding errors and identifying formerly unseen opportunities. Who would have believed that the Toyota fire would have resulted in improvements to the manufacture of the part involved and increased profitability for Toyota!

Further Implications for Leaders...

A lament we hear more and more often at InterClass is how decision making in organizations is being crunched by the clock. Overt preparation for taking actions is nearly invisible. Leaders feel pressured to make decisions in the moment. No one seems to have time to fully listen to presentations of the problem or opportunity at hand. We view this relentless focus on speed as highly detrimental to the quality of the outcomes and the humanity of the processes by which decisions are made in our organizations. As Malcolm Gladwell documented in his best-seller, *Blink*, some people are particularly skilled at making decisions in the moment and bringing to bear years of tacit knowledge to do so. That said, we do not feel that this kind of thought process is appropriate to all types of decisions nor is it supportive of the diversity of decision-makers within our organizations. At InterClass we value diversity of thinking as the greatest guarantor of quality decision making within an organization. We believe that a quality decision is one that can be well implemented. Having a broad array of thinkers providing input to decision making often motivates a broader group of stakeholders to participate in implementation.

Leaders today often need to decide not to decide. And each leader should have at least three mechanisms that they habitually use to prepare to take action.

Methods can be as simple as

- Counting to ten, breathing deeply three times, and waiting for your mind to catch up to what you have heard
- Engaging in additional and alternative forms of discussion with others in the moment or later on
- Having external sources to reach out to when deliberating

All of these are examples of methods of preparation our members say they wish were more present in their organizations. But the sense of urgency to make the decision often wins out over putting more emphasis on preparing to make the decision. InterClass does see a lot of value in acceleration tools, like the "Have you considered" method described above, or GE's famous Workout, for making decisions. But tools like workout involve 30 days of preparation even though the decision is made by the sponsor "in the moment." Too often our members see decisions being made just like that—as snap decisions made so that the next agenda item can be tackled.

Leaders today often need to decide not to decide.

Reaching Consensus on Actions to Take

Here at InterClass we make our decisions through consensus. We never vote on a course of action. Instead, we discuss a topic until everyone feels that they are 80% in agreement and 100% on board. Sometimes as facilitators, we will bring a contentious issue to a head, but usually consensus is reached organically and clearly. When a decision appears to the facilitators to be bogged down, we surface the implications of not making a decision and summarize the potential choices and their implications. Sometimes this means we simply table the item, because there really is no urgency even if there is significant interest, in favor of moving on to our next topic for exploration. The most common place in the operation of InterClass where decision making can get stuck is at the annual meeting where we decide on topics for our conferences for the next rolling 18 months. As the schedules in our participant organizations tighten, we find ourselves limited to 1 to 3 full conferences a year. This means that we often have more potatoes (topics) then we have bags (conferences) to put them in. This is where InterClass staff has had to bring things to a head by creating "what if" scenarios for the implications to each member's business of prioritizing one topic over another. This process usually enables the group to set their priorities through consensus.

Dialogue & Talking Stick

In our sessions, there are two primary methods we use for reaching consensus. The first method is dialogue. Dialogue in our events usually occurs in popcorn fashion, with participants speaking as they are moved to do so—speaking up at random around the room. This is particularly effective when we have more than 45 minutes for consensus building and are not at the end of a live or virtual session.

When we are closing an event, or want to be sure everyone is heard from specifically, and/or have less than 45 minutes, we use the Talking stick from the Native American tradition. The talking stick is a physical object—while the tradition calls for it to be an actual stick, it can take any form that's easily handled. We've used rubber balls, Halloween gourds, and paperweights, as well as beautifully crafted talking sticks designed just for that purpose. In a talking stick ceremony, the group will form a circle, while one person (often the facilitator) holds the stick and speaks. Then, he or she either hands it to someone else at their request or may hand it to the next person, and so it travels around the circle. It is perfectly acceptable to "pass"—that is, remain silent, when one's turn arrives.

Usually each speaker has a time limitation, never more than two minutes per person, and there is a time keeper. Sometimes the instructions are that you need to answer a specific question in only one sentence. Sometimes, when we have only a very short window at the end of a session, we will ask participants to 'fill in the blank' in a sentence with only one word. Consensus usually emerges organically. Sometimes facilitators help summarize, but this is rarely necessary. Also as will be discussed in the next chapter, consensus often does not need to appear in the room during a session. All InterClass sessions are documented so that the consensus developed in a dialogue or talking stick exercise appears transparently in the notes.

Implications for Leaders...

Using consensus as a method of decision making varies in popularity across organizations, geographies, and cultures. It works well in InterClass meetings because our context and content makes it less likely that participants will develop potentially polarizing fixed positions. Also, it's worth noting that at InterClass we are not making life or death decisions. Leaders who are constantly taking action of lesser and greater importance need to contemplate the mix of decision making and input gathering techniques they use. They need to identify what styles work best for them as individuals and for their organizations. It is essential that follow through occur, whatever techniques are employed. There is nothing more demoralizing to an organization than to go through an input process that is later ignored. Using a variety of decision-making and input gathering methods can add to the quality of the results and inclusiveness of the processes but only if all of the methods are skillfully handled by the leader and result in something tangible.

It is important for leaders to remember finishing the implementation of a decision, no matter how long it takes, does not fully realize the benefits available to the organization. Leaders need to ensure that their organizations learn from their actions and that measurement and communication of results occur. This does not require long drawn out decision-making audits. As the U.S. Army has demonstrated, immediate review after an initiative offers the best data and the most efficient analysis. This method is called after action reviews. The key questions answered by an after action review are what happened, why it happened, and how it can be done better. AARs include both participants and those responsible for a project or initiative. Whether implemented in the form of a formal AAR or not, immediate post-implementation reviews offer fruits of motivation and learning that can significantly benefit future initiatives.

POST CONFERENCE

The InterClass learning experience does not end with the close of a conference; InterClass assists in harvesting reflections and applying wisdom accrued during conferences.

Conference Process is Non-Linear

The different components of the InterClass process often appear in our conferences in a linear fashion. However, when viewed as a whole, we can see they actually function in a continuous circle where the first and last components (Post Conference and Disengage to Engage and Unit of One) flow into each other.

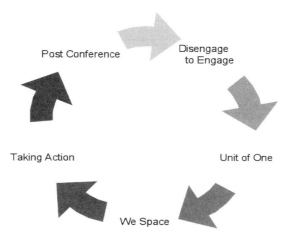

Post conference processes include activities that:

- participants do on their own usually with some preparatory work by InterClass staff
- are begun during the conference and continue after the conference, usually within the InterClass virtual network and/or conference calls
- participants/members do with their teams back at home and then bring back to the virtual network.

InterClass Official Conference Notes

Examples of activities participants do on their own include reviewing the notes created by InterClass staff that summarize each of our conferences. These notes differ somewhat from conference to conference but usually include participant quotes, conference content, and results of InterClass processes such as the knowledge café.

Notes from Individual Consultancies

Some notes are provided immediately after the conference, especially those from individual consultancies and "Have you considered…?" exercises. This information is often put to use right away by participants. Other more comprehensive conference notes tend to be delivered three to six weeks later. Our staff has often debated this timing. We have found it is useful to provide participants an opportunity to disengage from the conference before they reengage with the topic through our notes. Disengaging enables our members to gain yet another level of insights from the notes. Sometimes these insights develop simply because a reader finds a participant quote they had missed during the conference. The elapsed time enables additional company-specific information, such as project results, to surface and provide a new lens on conference topics.

In the past, when we've delivered notes right away, we tended to have fewer post-conference interactions—fewer questions were forwarded to us and fewer follow-up conference ideas were generated. The notes are a Unit-of-One-like activity in that they lead to an interaction between the self and a past experience, in the present state. They also involve disengaging to engage as distance from the conference is required before participants can again deeply engage about the event and its topic. This demonstrates what we mean about these stages of the InterClass conference process flowing into each other.

In-Conference Techniques to Generate Post-Conference Conversations

We also have several methods during a conference to encourage and make specific interactions that happen among participants between events. This most often takes the form of creating participant posters, one per participant, during the conference. Each poster features a participant's picture, name, company, title, and contact information, as well as their "offers" of assistance relative to conference topics and their "requests" for assistance. Participants usually create their own posters, which enhances their ideas and identity. The accuracy of the posters enables participants to create conversations on their own driven by the urgency of their requests and the motivation to share their offers. Sometimes we have time in a conference to create formal dance cards where participants meet with each other for multiple five minute slots during a 30-minute period to begin their offers and requests conversations. We find that dance cards do generate more follow-up activities after the conference.

Collecting the individual wisdom achieved during each conference is an essential part of our follow-up. We reinforce journaling all through our conferences and often gather answers to specific questions during the last few hours of each session. The questions focus on helping participants gather the insights from the conference that are most important to them and their work. This kind of information by definition cannot be collected until the conference is almost over, so there is little time to process these insights during conference time. Instead, the raw data often appears on our website and a processed synthesis is created, with the insights offered by time to disengage, in the meeting notes. We often receive the most comments on this portion of the meeting notes.

Live-Withs

An example of an activity we have used with the entire participant pool post conference involves a technique called "live-withs," created by Michael Ray, a professor at the Stanford University Graduate School of Business. InterClass delivered a combination of multiple conference calls and virtual network commentaries to support the InterClass network in exploring Michael Ray's concepts. These concepts offer insights into your own emotional intelligence. They are rules of thumb to be practiced and journaled so they can be called upon when needed in your life and work. An example is, "Have no expectations: If at first you don't succeed, surrender." For a week, instead of trying to manage meetings and control other situations, participants in this live-with stopped trying to change the course of events—they allowed the meeting or situation to just go where it was going. Participants wrote about their experiences and insights in their journals and shared their learnings in weekend conference calls. Individuals learned to increase the variations in their own behaviors by observing how much they "try" to control interactions. They learned to pay attention to their own emotional cues and note when they may be trying "too hard" to reach a desired conclusion. Other examples of Michael Ray's rules of thumb that were practiced this way included:

- Silence the voice of judgment, create curiosity
- All yes or no answers
- Pay attention
- Ask dumb questions
- Do only what you love and love what you do
- Don't think about it
- Be ordinary (show up and be present).

The power of these exercises is in the way they are reinforced over time, something that cannot be achieved within the limited timeframe of a conference. Participants found that repeated iterations over a longer period triggered real transformations in their behaviors, as well as in the behaviors of those around them. The results were significant qualitative differences in the outcome of their work. Several participants also reported that the live-with process led to expanding self-awareness—a benefit that meant as much, if not more, to their personal life and family than to work.

The live-with exercises could be seen as Unit of One exercises as the individuals were enacting these new behaviors back on the job on their own. Here too, though, the circle continues in post conference past the Unit of One into the "We Space." The sharing that occurred among participants, in sharing their live-with experiences in weekly conference calls, represents activities in the we space.

Those Who Can't Attend Conference Still Participate

Unfortunately, not everyone who wants to come to a meeting can, so it has been very useful to continue the circle of processes outside of actual conferences. Even when not attending, members can experience several processes in the circle. Often members unable to attend interact significantly through the conference notes. Some of the phone conversations around conference notes have yielded some of the deepest interactions we've had with members and have allowed them to meet many of their needs despite having missed our conference.

The notes also represent one of the key ways that attendees work with other members of their organizations. The notes are usually created in PowerPoint to make it easy to select slides, reorder, and annotate. Sometimes participants only e-mail around one slide, but the conversation that develops and is fed back to the InterClass staff or a design team heightens the breadth and depth of our understanding of a topic.

Action planning exercises are among the most powerful deliverables an InterClass conference can produce. Conference situations do not often allow time for in-depth planning, but when we have been able to help people lay out their intentions decisively, a clear path to more detailed planning became obvious to them. One of our favorite stories about this is an eight-year-long tale. At one of our conferences in Minneapolis we were lucky to have Gail Taylor of MG Taylor transform our environment into a highly effective collaborative space. One of our longtime members saw a need for creating dedicated spaces for doing work in a collaborative and accelerated fashion at the federal agency at which he worked. He spent the next eight years selling the idea and then building multiple centers in strategic locations across the country. The feedback loop to all of the other InterClass staff, participants, and members has been incredibly useful and illuminating on how our physical environments can help or hinder our work. When you have a really good idea, persevere!

Lessons for Leaders on Post- Activities

Follow-Up

One lesson we've learned from the post-conference process that leaders can bring forward in their daily work is the importance of follow-up. Meetings are needed, especially for building consensus, planning, and validating actions taken, but they are not usually where the true accomplishments of business really take place. The real accomplishments happen with our customers and our field staff in execution mode. If we do not follow up on commitments from meetings, how do we know if they were ever executed? An old and (we feel) true adage dating back to the work of Frederick Taylor is that you get more of any behavior to which you pay attention. If you take the time to ask about the status of a deliverable committed to in your meetings, then you will see these commitments executed on a consistent basis.

Timely Collection & Processing of Wisdom

Leaders can also learn from the effort InterClass makes to immediately collect and later process wisdom. Our race for efficiency and habit of multi-tasking, often make us feel most successful when we complete a meeting in the shortest amount of time possible, but does this lead to the best outcome? The collection of the insights at an InterClass conference rarely takes more than 10 minutes on the participants' part. The InterClass staff invest considerably more time in generating the questions that will elicit the most insightful responses from participants and that is precisely what leaders need to consider: How to frame powerful questions that generate insightful responses. By knowing what they want to get out of a meeting, and using their own time to get at these intentions ahead of time, leaders can gain efficiency and gather wisdom. The habit of ending meetings with summaries of what has been agreed to can be enhanced by adding a twist: Ask everyone (or some portion of the participants in larger meetings) for a closing insight or a learning from the process. The key is to ask a question that will ensure wisdom on the topic is not left unspoken. Gathering wisdom in this way enables us to leverage meetings beyond the present topic and apply that wisdom to the unknown that lies ahead.

Know Your Team Well

Another lesson for leaders concerns knowing what team members need and can offer. It never fails that when we do poster profiles someone who has been a member for many years places on their poster some experience or expertise that even those who know that individual well are surprised to learn. So often in work we do not have the time to fully understand the competencies of our co-workers. Making that time pays off—this is at the core of effective business networking. The ability to be within two phone calls of any data you need is a powerful asset. It's just as significant to know who you can turn to on the team to get needed input, during a meeting or while on a critical work assignment.

Knowing the abilities of those around you and the abilities of the people they can further link you to enables speed, agility, and accuracy in gathering and applying wisdom.

This also defines the core deliverable of the InterClass network.

Networking may appear to be an exercise of chaos, but it is an asset that can be programmatically leveraged for its wisdom. This is true whether the network is a leader's own team, their supply chain, or all their stakeholders. Knowing the abilities of those around you and the abilities of the people they can further link you to enables speed, agility, and accuracy in gathering and applying wisdom. This also defines the core deliverable of the InterClass network.